Silent Spring

by Rachel Carson

Level 5

Adopted by Raina Ruth Nakamura

IBC パブリッシング

はじめに

　ラダーシリーズは、「はしご (ladder)」を使って一歩一歩上を目指すように、学習者の実力に合わせ、無理なくステップアップできるよう開発された英文リーダーのシリーズです。

　リーディング力をつけるためには、繰り返したくさん読むこと、いわゆる「多読」がもっとも効果的な学習法であると言われています。多読では、「1. 速く 2. 訳さず英語のまま 3. なるべく辞書を使わず」に読むことが大切です。スピードを計るなど、速く読むよう心がけましょう（たとえば TOEIC® テストの音声スピードはおよそ 1 分間に 150 語です）。そして 1 語ずつ訳すのではなく、英語を英語のまま理解するくせをつけるようにします。こうして読み続けるうちに語感がついてきて、だんだんと英語が理解できるようになるのです。まずは、ラダーシリーズの中からあなたのレベルに合った本を選び、少しずつ英文に慣れ親しんでください。たくさんの本を手にとるうちに、英文書がすらすら読めるようになってくるはずです。

《本シリーズの特徴》

- 中学校レベルから中級者レベルまで5段階に分かれています。自分に合ったレベルからスタートしてください。
- クラシックから現代文学、ノンフィクション、ビジネスと幅広いジャンルを扱っています。あなたの興味に合わせてタイトルを選べます。
- 巻末のワードリストで、いつでもどこでも単語の意味を確認できます。レベル1、2では、文中の全ての単語が、レベル3以上は中学校レベル外の単語が掲載されています。
- カバーにヘッドホーンマークのついているタイトルは、オーディオ・サポートがあります。ウェブから購入／ダウンロードし、リスニング教材としても併用できます。

《使用語彙について》

レベル1：中学校で学習する単語約1000語

レベル2：レベル1の単語＋使用頻度の高い単語約300語

レベル3：レベル1の単語＋使用頻度の高い単語約600語

レベル4：レベル1の単語＋使用頻度の高い単語約1000語

レベル5：語彙制限なし

Contents

読み始める前に

　『Silent Spring（沈黙の春）』は、生物学者レイチェル・カーソンが1962年に発表した、化学物質の乱用が自然環境を破壊し、生物多様性が失われていることを指摘した本です。この本は、世界的な環境問題への警鐘として注目され、多くの人々に読まれてきました。本書は、英語学習者向けに、原文を短く、やさしい英語に書き改めたものですが、本文中に多くの化学物質や化合物の名称、動植物名が登場します。本書をスムーズに読んで楽しんでいただくために、あらかじめ下記のリストに目を通していただくことをお勧めします。

【主な化学物質、化合物】

2,4-D	2,4-ジクロロフェノキシ酢酸	除草剤の一種で、双子葉植物に対して強い除草効果がある
additive	添加物、添加剤	着色剤や香料、防腐剤など、食品やガソリンなどに添加される物質のこと
aldrin	アルドリン	有機塩素系の農薬で、特に害虫駆除に用いられた
amitrol	アミトロール	除草剤の一種。農地や産業用地、鉄道の線路などでの雑草の管理に利用される
arsenic	ヒ素	元素記号がAsで、原子番号が33の元素。自然界には主に硫化鉱石として存在し、半導体や殺虫剤、木材防腐剤などに利用される
ATP (adenosine triphosphate)	アデノシン三リン酸	生物学的なエネルギーの基本的な分子
attractant	誘引物質、誘引薬	生物が他の生物に対して好奇心や興味を持ちやすいように作られた物質のこと

benzene	ベンゼン	有機合成の出発物質として、プラスチック、合成ゴム、染料、医薬品、農薬などの製造に使われる有機化合物
benzene hexachloride	ベンゼンヘキサクロライド	有機塩素系の化学物質で、殺虫剤として広く使用された
carbohydrate	炭水化物、糖質	炭素、水素、酸素の原子からなる有機化合物で、生物の主要な構成要素とエネルギー源の一つ
carbon tetrachloride	四塩化炭素	無機化合物で、有機溶媒として広く使用された
chlordane	クロルダン	有機塩素系の農薬で、害虫駆除などに広く使用された
chloride	塩化物	塩化ナトリウムや塩化水素など、塩素が他の元素や原子団と結合してできる化合物のこと
chlorinated hydrocarbon	塩素化炭化水素	炭素と水素から構成される炭化水素に、塩素が結合した化合物
chlorine	塩素	原子番号17の元素で、元素記号はCl。常温常圧では特有の臭いを有する黄緑色の気体で、強い漂白・殺菌作用を持つ
chloroform	クロロホルム	かつて麻酔薬として使用された有機化合物
CIPC	クロロイソプロピルカルバミン酸エステル	IPCよりも土壌吸着性が高く、雑草の発芽を抑制する効果がある
DDD	2,4-ジクロロジフェニルジクロロエタン	DDTの構造中で、トリクロロメチル基がジクロロメチル基となったもの。殺虫剤の一種
DDE	ジクロロジフェニルジクロロエチレン	DDTが環境中で分解された際に生成される代謝物の一つ。農業用途や疾病媒介生物の駆除などに使用された
DDT	ジクロロジフェニルトリクロロエタン	広く使用されていた有機塩素系の農薬で、主に殺虫剤として知られる
dieldrin	ダイエルドリン	有機塩素系の農薬で、特に害虫駆除のために広く使用された

endrin	エンドリン	有機塩素系の農薬で、特に害虫駆除に使用された
fluoride	フッ化物	フッ素と他の元素との化合物
heptachlor	ヘプタクロール	有機塩素系の農薬で、害虫駆除などに広く使用された
hexachloride	六塩化物	元素が六つのクロロ (chloro) 原子と結合している化合物
hydrocarbon	炭化水素	炭素と水素だけでできた化合物の総称
IPC	イソプロピルカルバミン酸エステル	イネ科雑草に選択的に効果がある除草剤
lindane	リンデン	クロロベンゼン系の有機塩素化合物で、農薬および殺虫剤として使用された
malathion	マラチオン	有機リン系の農薬で、主に殺虫剤として使用、昆虫やダニなどの害虫に対して効果的とされる
methane	メタン	天然ガスの主要成分
methyl chloride	メチルクロライド	メタンに塩素原子が結合した有機塩素化合物
mineral compound	無機化合物	植物と動物以外の物質から成る化合物
nitrate	硝酸塩	nitrateとは、窒素原子が3つの酸素原子と結合し、1つの負の電荷を持つイオンやその塩を指す。また、このイオンが他の陽イオンと結合した化合物を「硝酸塩」と呼ぶ
nitrogen oxide	酸化窒素、窒素酸化物	窒素と酸素からなる無機化合物の総称。一酸化窒素 (NO)、二酸化窒素 (NO_2)、亜酸化窒素 (N_2O) などがある
organic phosphate	有機リン酸塩	有機物にリン酸基が結合した化合物
organic phosphorus	有機リン	有機化合物の中にリンが含まれる形態

oxide	酸化物	酸素とそれより電気陰性度が小さい元素からなる化合物の総称
parathion	パラチオン	有機リン系の農薬で、殺虫剤として使用され、昆虫に対して神経毒性を発揮する
pentachlorophenol	ペンタクロロフェノール	除草剤として使用された。略称はpenta
phenol	フェノール	無色の結晶性固体。殺菌剤、合成樹脂、医薬品の原料
phosphate	リン酸塩	リン酸の塩類の総称
phosphorus	リン	原子番号が15番の元素で、元素記号はP。生命に必須の元素であり、DNAやRNA、ATPなどの重要な生体分子の構成成分。また、肥料や洗剤などの工業製品にも利用される
pyrethrin	ピレスリン	菊の花から抽出される天然の植物性殺虫剤
rotenone	ロテノン	植物由来の化合物で、魚毒や農薬として使用されることがある
selenium	セレン	化学記号Seで表される原子番号34の元素。たんぱく質や酵素の構成要素として、植物や動物の生命活動に必要なミネラルの一つ
sodium arsenite	亜ヒ酸ナトリウム	有毒な無機化合物。殺虫剤や防カビ剤、木材の保存剤として使用された
strontium 90	ストロンチウム90	核爆発や原子力発電などの核反応に由来して発生する放射性物質
systemic insecticide	浸透殺虫剤	植物に吸収され、害虫に対して効果を発揮する農薬の一種
toxaphene	トキサフェン	農業用途で使用された有機塩素系の農薬
triphosphate	三リン酸塩	リン酸が3つ結合したイオンで、ATPなどの生物学的な分子に見られる構造の一部

【主な動植物】

algae	藻(類)
American elm	アメリカニレ
antelope	レイヨウ、アンテロープ《角を持つウシ科の偶蹄類》
aphid	アブラムシ
balsam	バルサムモミ
bedbug	トコジラミ
blackfly	ブユ
body lice	ヒトジラミ
brook trout	カワマス
brown thrasher	チャイロツグミモドキ
budworm	花や針葉樹の芽や葉を食べるガの幼虫
cabbage aphid	ダイコンアブラムシ
chrysanthemum	菊
cockroach	ゴキブリ
codling moth	コドリンガ
coyote	コヨーテ
cranberry	ツルコケモモ、クランベリー
Douglas fir	ダグラスファー、ベイマツ
fiddler crab	シオマネキ
fire ant	ヒアリ
flea	ノミ
flour moth	コクガの一種
fruit fly	ミバエ
fungus	真菌、菌類《複数形はfungi》
gnat	ブユ
grebe	カイツブリ
grouse	ライチョウ
gull	カモメ

gypsy moth	マイマイガ
hemlock	アメリカツガ（またはカナダツガ）
honeybee	ミツバチ
housefly	イエバエ
Japanese beetle	マメコガネ
jay	カケス
Kaibab deer	カイバブ鹿
Klamath weed	セイヨウオトギリソウ《通称St. John's Wort》
ladybug	テントウムシ
mantis	カマキリ
melon fly	ウリミバエ
mite	ダニ
moose	ヘラジカ、ムース
muskrat	マスクラット《ネズミ科の雑食性の動物》
pheasant	キジ
pronghorn antelope	プロングホーン、エダツノレイヨウ
puma	ピューマ
quail	ウズラ
raccoon	アライグマ
rat flea	ネズミノミ
red ant	赤アリ
rhubarb	ダイオウ、大黄《タデ科の多年草》
robin	コマドリ
root borer	根食い虫《植物の根に穴をあけて食害する昆虫》
root weevil	ルートウィービル《ゾウムシ上科に属する甲虫》
ryania	カワラケツメイ《根の成分が、昆虫に対して毒性を発揮》

sage grouse	キジオライチョウ
sagebrush	ヤマヨモギ《アメリカ西部の乾燥地帯に広く分布する低木》
salt marsh mosquito	塩性湿地の蚊
screw-worm fly	ラセンウジバエ《幼虫が生きた動物の肉を食う害虫》
shrew	トガリネズミ
songbird	鳴禽類《スズメ亜目の鳥の総称》
spider mite	ハダニ
spruce	トウヒ《マツ科トウヒ属の常緑針葉樹の総称》
spruce budworm	スプルースバドワーム《針葉樹林で発生する毛虫の一種》
St. John's Wort	セイヨウオトギリソウ《ヨーロッパやアジアを原産とするハーブ》
starling	ムクドリ
sugar beet	サトウダイコン
tick	ダニ
tsetse fly	ツェツェバエ《アフリカに生息する吸血性のハエ》
weed	雑草
western brebe	クビナガカイツブリ
wild turkey	ワイルド・ターキー《七面鳥の野生種》
yellow jacket	スズメバチ

Silent Spring

A Fable for Tomorrow

There once was a town in the middle of America where animals, plants, and people all lived together in harmony. Many farms were placed like a checkerboard across the land. In spring, white fluffy clouds floated above the green squares of the farms. In fall, the oak and maple trees looked like fire in the forest of green pine trees. Through the fields and forest, foxes and deer walked silently.

Even in winter birds came to feed on the berries and dried weeds sticking up out of the snow. This place was famous for its wide variety of birds, and travelers came from all over to watch them. They also came to fish for trout in the streams that came down cold and clear from the hills.

Suddenly, though, a strange disease settled over the area. Chickens, cows, and sheep became sick and died. People, including children, were also getting mysterious illnesses that the doctors could not explain.

Outside it was oddly quiet. Where had the birds gone? A few birds could still be seen, but they were too sick to fly. The sound of robins, doves, and jays had gone silent in this strange springtime.

The rooftops, fields, and streams were covered with a white powder, as if it had been sprinkled by a witch flying over the town. But this was no evil spell or witchcraft. The people had done it themselves.

Though this town doesn't exist, many places

in America and other countries have experienced parts of the disaster described here. This imagined tragedy could become reality for all of us. What has made the voices of spring silent? This book will try to explain exactly that.

2

The Obligation to Endure

Throughout the history of life on earth, animals and plants have been shaped by the environment. However, in the past twenty-five years, one species—man—has become able to change the environment. The most frightening way this happens is through chemicals polluting the air, land, and water. The effects of this pollution can be impossible to reverse. For example, strontium 90, which is released from nuclear explosions, comes down to earth as rain or fallout that gets into soil, plants, and human bones. In the same way, chemicals sprayed on farms, forests, and gardens enter insects and smaller wildlife, passing up through the chain of life with deadly results. As Albert Schweitzer has said, "Man can hardly even recognize the devils of his own creation."

Albert Schweitzer

Nature itself has the power to harm, as in the case of the radiation in sunlight that burns our skin. But the earth has had hundreds of millions of years to adjust and balance itself with both the benefits and dangers of the sun and other elements. In the modern world, however, things are changing too fast for a balance to be found. Chemicals created in laboratories are being released at the rate of 500 per year in the United States. Humans and animals do not have time to adjust to this continuous stream of poison.

Chemical sprays made to kill insects have become extremely common. They should be called 'biocides' rather than 'insecticides' because they can also silence birds and poison fish. There is an endless circle because the sprays lose their effect on insects and stronger chemicals need to be used. Can anyone really believe it is possible to use these sprays without making the earth unsuitable for other forms of life?

The reasons given for using deadly insecticides usually include farm production. But our real problem is overproduction, rather than underproduction. The American taxpayers are paying farmers more than a billion dollars a year for the cost of the surplus-food storage program.

Of course, I am not saying that insects do not need to be controlled in some way. I am asking for methods to be used that do not destroy humans along with a few species of insects.

The current insect problem has come about due to our modern way of life. Long before humans took over the earth, many varieties of insects lived and changed naturally. But now insects and humans are fighting for two main reasons: food supply and disease. Early farmers did not have big problems with them. But the modern style of farming makes it easy for specific insect populations to increase quickly. When they grow only one type of food crop, such as wheat, farmers have to deal with a larger number of insects that live on wheat. If farmers grew a different type of plant along with the wheat, fewer wheat-eating insects would be found.

Another problem is the introduction of foreign plants into a country. Almost 200,000 plants from other countries have been introduced to the US. Along with these new plants come insects that are their enemies. In their home environment, these enemies are not as deadly because they also have natural enemies. In the new environment, however, there are often fewer enemies to keep the introduced insect population down.

There is an alternative to just getting rid of certain plants or animals. We need some basic knowledge of the animals and their relationship to their original environment so we can keep a balance and limit the possibility of diseases and other problems.

This basic knowledge is available, but we don't use it. No one is listening to the ecologists who are giving advice on topics they've studied. We use deadly chemicals because we think there are no other choices, but in fact there are many other options.

I don't propose that these chemicals should never be used, but they need to be used with care and by people who know what the risks are. Future generations will not approve of our current behavior, which shows little concern for the natural world that supports all life.

Information about the threat is very hard to find. We are now in an era of specialists who are often unaware of any problem outside their own specialties. We also live in a time where a business's right to make money is rarely questioned. Whenever people protest, the industry tells half-truths to calm them. We urgently need to end these false answers. We need to have all the facts so we can make a decision about whether to continue on this present road. As Jean Rostand says, "The obligation to endure gives us the right to know."

Jean Rostand

3

Deadly Chemicals

Since artificial pesticides were first released some twenty years ago, they have found their way into every type of life, from the smallest creature to the greatest, including men, women, and possibly unborn children. They have polluted rivers and the groundwater below the earth. These chemicals do not wash away completely; part of them stays and can last for years.

Many of these man-made products are a result of World War II. Scientists who were developing chemical weapons during the war found that the chemicals killed insects. These new chemicals are quite different from traditional pesticides before the war. Before the war, pesticides were made from natural mineral compounds, such as arsenic and copper, or plants like chrysanthemums and tobacco. By creating pesticides in laboratories, scientists have unintentionally released products far more powerful than before. These are not just poisonous to humans, but can change the body in deadly ways.

The number of these deadly chemicals is astonishing. In the US alone, the production of pesticides rose from 124,259,000 pounds in 1947 to 637,666,000 pounds in 1960. The value of these products was over a quarter of a billion dollars. And this was only the beginning for the industry.

Arsenic is still being used in some weed killers and pesticides today. Arsenic is found in small amounts in metals, volcanoes, the ocean, and spring water. It has been a favorite method of murder from long ago to the present day and was the first type of dangerous material found to cause cancer. Beekeeping in

Wilhelm Hueper

the southern US has almost completely died out because arsenic was sprayed on cotton plants. Dr. Hueper of the National Cancer Institute has said that it is "supremely careless" to use insecticides with arsenic.

Yet the new insecticides are even more deadly. There are two major groups of chemicals. The first is the "chlorinated hydrocarbons," of which DDT is the most well known. The second is the organic phosphorus insecticides, of which malathion and parathion are the most familiar. Both groups are built with carbon atoms, which are the basic building blocks of every living thing. If we want to understand these deadly chemicals, we must see what they are made of and how they have been changed into agents of death.

Carbon atoms have an almost unlimited ability to bond with each other and with other elements. Protein, fat, carbohydrates, enzymes, and vitamins all start with the basic element of carbon.

Marsh gas, or methane, is made by the natural process of living matter decaying from bacteria underwater. Methane is simply a combination of carbon and hydrogen.

$$\begin{array}{ccc} H & & H \\ & \diagdown \diagup & \\ & C & \\ & \diagup \diagdown & \\ H & & H \end{array}$$

Scientists have been able to combine carbon with other elements, like chlorine, to make methyl chloride.

Chloroform is made with carbon, hydrogen, and three chlorine atoms.

Carbon tetrachloride, a common cleaning product, is made as chloroform above, but without the hydrogen atom.

These variations of chlorine and hydrocarbon give only a small hint into the complex world of hydrogen and carbon. Chemists can work with rings or chains of carbon to make a completely different product. It is these complex combinations of elements that have given us a large group of very powerful poisons.

DDT was first made by a German chemist  in 1874, but it didn't become an insecticide until 1939. Paul Müller was the Swiss scientist who made DDT into a product that could help farmers win the war against insects. He won the Nobel Prize for his discovery.

Paul Müller

DDT is so common now that it seems harmless in most people's minds. One event that led people to believe DDT causes no damage to humans was the DDT spraying of soldiers and prisoners in wartime to fight lice. In its powdered form, DDT does not easily get into human skin. But dissolved in oil, as it usually is, DDT is definitely poisonous.

Just a tiny amount of DDT can be harmful. We refer to it in parts per million, that is, one part DDT to a million parts oil. However, even in such small amounts, DDT has been shown to be harmful to animals. With five parts per million, the liver can be damaged. DDT and other chemicals build up and cannot easily be gotten rid of, so they can poison organs quite easily in small amounts.

One of the most evil parts of DDT and other chemicals is how they are passed through the food chain. For example, hay is sprayed with DDT, and then is made into food for chickens. The chickens lay eggs containing DDT. Or the hay is fed to cows and the DDT level in cows' milk becomes 3 parts per million. But the butter from those cows has 65 parts per million because the poison is stored in the cows' fat.

Insecticide has also been found in human breast milk. Other harmful chemicals can affect the baby in the womb, which means they already have these poisonous substances in their bodies when they are born. Furthermore, babies and young children cannot fight the effects as easily as adults can.

The US Food and Drug Administration (FDA) said in 1950 that the danger of DDT has been underestimated. We are in a completely new situation, and no one knows what the results will be.

Now let's turn to other common types of insecticides. Chlordane is like DDT in many ways, but has some special effects that DDT does not. It can easily get into human skin, can be breathed in, and can get into the stomach through food. Even when an animal eats food with only 2.5 parts per million, it can be stored in the animal's fat at 75 parts per million. One man using a mixture of chlordane and water accidentally spilled some on his hand. He got sick within 40 minutes and was dead before medical help could arrive.

A type of chlordane called heptachlor can be stored in large amounts in fat. Even with just 1/10 of 1 part per million of heptachlor in food, much more can be found in the body. It can also change into a different chemical in soil, in plants, and in animals. This different chemical was found in birds and was four times as poisonous as the original chlordane.

There is a special group of hydrocarbons that were found to cause hepatitis in the mid-1930s. Three insecticides belong to this group: dieldrin, aldrin, and endrin. Dieldrin is about five times as poisonous as DDT when swallowed, but 40 times as deadly when applied to the skin. When birds like quail and pheasants were tested, dieldrin was found to be 40 to 50 times as poisonous as DDT. The World Health Organization discovered just how deadly dieldrin is when they used it instead of DDT in malaria control. The workers who were spraying started shaking severely, and several died.

Aldrin is also highly poisonous. It affects the livers and kidneys of animals. An amount of aldrin the size of an aspirin can kill more than 400 quail. Aldrin, like most of the chemicals in this group, also affects an animal's ability to make healthy babies. A small amount of aldrin was given to pheasants who laid only a few eggs. The chicks from those eggs soon died. Baby rats whose mothers had been given aldrin died within three days. No one knows if the same effect could be seen in human beings, but this chemical has been sprayed from airplanes over houses and farms.

Endrin is the most poisonous of all the chlorinated hydrocarbons. It is closely related to dieldrin but is five times stronger. It is 30 times as poisonous to fish as DDT is, and it is 300 times as poisonous to some birds. A sad case of endrin poisoning happened in Venezuela. An American family moved there and found cockroaches in their house. They took their dog and one-year-old baby outside and sprayed the house at 9 a.m. Then they washed the floors and brought the dog and baby back inside in the mid-afternoon. Within an hour, the dog was dead and by 10 p.m. the baby started shaking strongly and fainted. Though he was treated in a New York hospital for three months, he is now a vegetable, unable to see or hear. There is no hope for his recovery.

The second main group of insecticides, the organic phosphates, are some of the most poisonous chemicals in the world. Children have died just from touching an empty bag that had once held it. In another case, one child died from breathing the parathion his father was spraying on potatoes and his cousin died after touching the spraying hose.

Parathion is one of the most commonly used and also one of the most dangerous. Honeybees react wildly and try to clean themselves crazily after coming in contact with parathion. They are close to death within thirty minutes. In Finland, people use parathion for suicide and in California 200 cases of accidental parathion poisoning are reported yearly. In other parts of the world, the death rate yearly from parathion is surprising: 100 deaths in India, 67 in Syria and an average of 336 in Japan.

In spite of this, some 7,000,000 pounds of parathion are sprayed on American farms each year. The only factor that saves us from killing ourselves off completely is the fact that parathion and other phosphates break down quickly. This does not mean they do not cause harm after time has passed, however. A case in California showed that one-third of an orange-picking crew had to go to the hospital after handling oranges that had been sprayed with parathion two-and-a-half weeks earlier. Even six months after spraying, small amounts of parathion have been found in oranges.

Malathion, another organic phosphate, is as common as DDT since it is advertised for safe use in gardens and houses. Humans are somewhat safe from malathion poisoning because our livers protect us from it. Unfortunately, when combined with other phosphates, malathion becomes 50 times more harmful than it is by itself. If a sprayer uses malathion one week and a different chemical the next week, the combination of the chemicals can be dangerous. It could also affect someone eating a salad where small amounts of more than one chemical could be found on each piece of food.

Though research has hardly begun on the subject of medications combined with parathion and malathion, it is known that these phosphates increase the deadliness of such medicines as muscle relaxers and sleeping pills.

There is also a strange group of insecticides called 'systemic insecticides.' Unlike ordinary insecticides, which are just on the surface of the plant, systemic insecticides make every part of the plant poisonous. They were discovered when scientists found that wheat growing in soil containing selenium was not attacked by aphids or spider mites. Now, seeds of various common plants like cotton, peas, beans, and sugar beets are painted with insecticides so that when they grow, they are poisonous to their enemies. However, when the honey made by bees that visited such plants was tested, it was also poisoned with the insecticide.

aphid

spider mite

Systemic products are even being used outside of farming. You can give your dog a pill that is said to make its blood poisonous to fleas.

So far, we have been focusing on poisons that kill insects. But what of chemicals that kill unwanted plants, or weed killers? We have been told they aren't dangerous to animals, but unfortunately that is not true. Sodium arsenite, which is commonly used on roadsides, has killed many cows, as well as unknown numbers of wild animals. When used in lakes, sodium arsenite has even poisoned drinking water and made swimming impossible.

In England farmers began using arsenic sprays in their potato fields around 1951. The Ministry of Agriculture warned of the dangers of going into these fields, but unfortunately cows and other animals, including birds, could not understand these warnings. In 1959, when a farmer's wife died of arsenic poisoning from drinking water, the major English chemical companies stopped producing arsenic sprays and recalled all products already in stores. The UK government put limits on the use of these sprays. In 1961, Australia also banned these products. However, in the US there is no such ban.

One type of chemical called penta (short for pentachlorophenol) is often sprayed along railroad tracks. A deadly case of penta poisoning was reported in California. A sprayer in a cotton field was mixing oil with penta when he dropped the hose. He picked up the hose from the penta container with his bare hand and died the next day.

Two other types of weed killers are possibly even more dangerous. The cranberry weed killer known as amitrol is said to be less dangerous than other chemicals. But over time, it causes tumors in wildlife and possibly in humans. A second type of weed killer known as a 'mutagen' can change genes. We are, of course, horrified by the effects of radiation on genes. So how can we ignore the same effects from chemicals that are being sprayed widely in our environment?

Surface Water and Underground Seas

Water has become the most precious of all our natural resources. Because most of the earth's water is not usable for farming, drinking, or industry, we face serious shortages of it. However, our waterways are being polluted by radioactive waste from nuclear plants, laboratories, and hospitals, domestic waste from cities, and chemical waste from factories. Now we can add a new source to the list: dangerous sprays from farms, forests, fields, and gardens. The chemicals from these sprays cannot be identified or removed from drinking water by any current cleaning processes. One professor from the Massachusetts Institute of Technology stated to a committee in Congress, "What is the effect on the people? We don't know."

There are many examples of the effects on wildlife, however. In Pennsylvania, drinking water from an orchard area was tested on fish. They died of insecticide poisoning within four hours. In Alabama, water from sprayed cotton fields killed fish even after the water had gone through a cleaning process. A report by the U.S. Fish and Wildlife Service in 1960 stated that even 30 miles from the area being sprayed to control the spruce budworm, fish were poisoned by DDT.

eastern spruce budworm

It is not only local streams and rivers that are being poisoned. The chemicals from DDT and other pesticides can get into groundwater. Nature does not work in closed and separate compartments, and the earth's water is proof of this. Rain falls and goes down through the soil and rocks to a place that could be called an underground sea. This water is moving, in some places slowly and in other places more quickly. It sometimes comes to the surface as a spring or is found by digging a well. Because the earth's water is connected in this wide system, pollution of groundwater means pollution of water everywhere.

One of the earliest cases of poisoned groundwater happened in Colorado. In 1943, a facility near Denver started making war materials. Eight years later the facility was rented by an oil company to make insecticides. Before the insecticide production even began, however, nearby farmers reported their cows were sick and their plants were dying. Humans became sick too.

When the well water on the farms was tested, many chemicals, like chlorides, fluorides, and arsenic, were found. The war-materials facility had put its wastewater into holding ponds until it could be gotten rid of properly. It took seven to eight years for the chemicals in the ponds to travel underground to the nearest farm. It was not known how far the poison traveled after that.

Later, the chemical 2,4-D was found in the well water, even though the war-materials facility never used or produced it. This chemical had been formed while sitting outside in the ponds. When the original chemicals from the wastewater sat in the air and sunlight for many years, this new and very dangerous chemical was created.

The US Public Health Service fears that this type of chemical creation could be happening in many other places. It could happen when two or more chemicals come together or when radioactive waste combines with chemicals. It could create chemicals in ways that we cannot know or control.

Another example of poisoned water, this time above ground, happened in California. In 1960, animal refuge staff found dead birds along Tule Lake and the Lower Klamath River. They were all fish-eating birds, like herons and pelicans, grebes, and gulls. When tested, the birds and the fish from the lake all had DDD and DDE in their bodies. These chemicals were coming from farms upstream on the Upper Klamath River in Oregon. This was especially dangerous because three-quarters of all water birds that fly south for the winter pass through this area.

In another case in California, residents and fishermen of Clear Lake wanted to get rid of an annoying insect called the small gnat. DDD was chosen instead of DDT because it was supposed to be less danger-ous. In 1949, a small amount was

black fungus gnat

used, 1 part DDD to 70 million parts water. It did reduce the gnats, but the lake area was treated again in 1954 with 1 part DDD

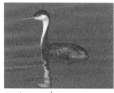

western grebe

to 50 million parts water. That winter, western grebes started to die, though no disease was found in them. In 1957, more grebes died and someone decided to look in the fatty parts of the birds' bodies. DDD in the amount of 1,600 parts per million was discovered.

How had the DDD levels become so high and so deadly? The fish were studied, and a picture of the problem was created. Starting from the lowest place on the food chain, plankton were found to have DDD in the amount of 5 parts per million. The fish that ate the plankton had 40–300 parts per million. Fish that ate meat had the highest amount of DDD—2,500 parts per million. This is how the food chain works. What happens to the lowest member of the chain gets passed up to the highest member.

An almost unbelievable fact was discovered later. No DDD was found in the lake water itself. It had all gone into the life in the lake. Even two years later, DDD was found in plankton, having been passed from generation to generation. The grebes declined from more than 100 pairs to about 30, and none of those had babies. In 1959 the California Department of Public Health banned DDD use in the lake.

Water has to be considered in terms of the chains of life it supports, from the smallest cells of plant plankton to fish, then to the bigger animals that eat the fish. Can we imagine that poisons we put in water will not enter these natural cycles?

This case shows us something that the public needs to think about. Is it okay to use dangerous chemicals to fix an "annoying" problem when the results can be deadly to all life? It doesn't matter if the chemical is mixed with large amounts of water. The amount of it grows as it moves up the food chain.

Soil

The thin layer of soil that covers the land affects humans and every other animal on earth. Without the soil, plants could not grow, and without plants, no animals could survive. The soil was made by the reactions between living and nonliving things a long time ago. Volcanoes, water, ice, moss—all these elements combined to create soil. Therefore, soil is not a dead thing; it is a place where many organisms come together to support the earth's green cover.

Soil is always changing as new materials are added and others break down and get washed away. There are also many chemical changes that involve air and water and create the conditions that plants need to grow. Soil depends on living things like bacteria, fungi, and algae. Just a teaspoon of soil can host billions of bacteria. Fungi and algae are less common, but also very important.

There are also other tiny organisms that have special tasks. For example, mites begin their lives in the fallen needles of spruce trees. These tiny insects eat almost the whole needle. The mites and other insects do a truly incredible job by eating a large amount of the leaves and other plant material on the forest floor.

Another amazing creature of the soil is the earthworm. Charles Darwin taught the world about the importance of earthworms in moving soil from below the surface to the top. He calculated

Charles Darwin

that earthworms could add an inch to an inch and a half to the soil in ten years. Of course, they also help keep the soil well drained, allowing the roots of plants to grow deep down.

So what happens to these tiny but mighty creatures of the soil when poisonous chemicals are introduced into their world? How is it possible to kill the 'bad' pests without killing any of the 'good' ones? Everyone, even scientists, seems to have ignored the ecology of the soil.

It's important to remember that pesticides stay in the soil not just for months, but for years. Aldrin, which was discussed before, has been shown to last four years. Toxaphene stays in sandy soil for ten years. Benzene hexachloride remains for at least eleven years and chlordane has been found twelve years after being sprayed on the ground.

Arsenic is nearly permanent in the soil. A study said that American tobacco grown from

1932 to 1952 showed a 300 percent increase in arsenic. Even after arsenic was taken out of sprays in the mid-1940s, it continued to be found in the ground.

Carrots absorb more insecticides than any other plant studied. In some cases, they were shown to have higher amounts of chemicals than the soil itself. In the future, farmers may have to test the soil before they plant anything. This is because even if they haven't been sprayed, the plants may get too much insecticide from the soil.

A baby food maker had trouble finding vegetables that had not been sprayed with poisonous chemicals. Sweet potatoes in California were found to have benzene hexachloride, which had been sprayed on the farm two years earlier. The baby food maker then tried to buy sweet potatoes from another farm in South Carolina. That farm's sweet potatoes also had been poisoned.

Finally, the baby food company bought sweet potatoes on the open market which was much more expensive.

Some insecticides affect sensitive plants like beans, wheat, and rye, causing the growth of

root weevil

seedlings to slow down. In 1955 some farmers growing hop in Washington and Idaho sprayed heptachlor to control insects called root weevils. Since then, the hop's vines have not been growing. Even five years after the first spraying, the soil still had enough heptachlor in it to keep the hop from growing properly.

As poisonous chemicals continue to build up in sprayed soil, we are almost certainly going to have trouble. In 1960 a group of scientists met to discuss the ecology of the soil. They said that using such powerful and poorly understood chemicals could mean the end of soil productivity.

6

Earth's Green Mantle

Plants provide what we and other animals need to survive. But we kill plants that we don't have uses for or that get in the way of the plants we're trying to grow. The weed killer business is booming.

One example of our unthinking destruction of nature is in the sagebrush lands of the western United States. There is a campaign there to kill the sage and replace it with grasslands

sagebrush

for cattle to feed on. This is a perfect example of people being unwilling to look at the history of the land. If we would only look closely at the story nature has to tell us, we would find important reasons to keep it as it is.

When the Rocky Mountains were raised up many millions of years ago, they created high plains and lower hills around them. This was a place of extreme climate: long winters and dry, hot summers. Finally, one type of plant evolved that combined all the factors needed to survive in this region. It was the low-growing sage, which could hold enough water in its small leaves to live through the dry summers. These plants attracted animals that evolved along with them. Two of these animals become perfectly adjusted to this area, the pronghorn antelope and the sage grouse, a type of wild chicken.

Sage gives the grouse a place to build its nest, as well as providing food. The antelope also eats the sage leaves, especially in winter, because the sage does not lose its leaves as other plants do.

pronghorn antelope

But this perfect balance of nature has been damaged by ranchers needing more grass for their cattle. They asked the government to get rid of the sage and plant grass instead. The

sage grouse

long-term effects of this sage removal are not known yet, but it is likely the antelope and sage grouse will disappear. A second terrible side effect comes from spraying to kill the sage. In the western state of Wyoming, 10,000 acres of sagelands were sprayed with herbicide. The willow trees near the rivers, which had given shade to moose, bear, and fish, were also killed. One writer went to the area a year after the spraying and found dead, leafless trees and no animals.

This type of tragedy is happening not only in the west, but in the northeast and southwest as well. Spraying of farmlands doubled in the 1950s, reaching 53 million acres by 1959. And that doesn't include all the private yards, parks, and golf courses also being sprayed with herbicides.

Another attack on nature by chemicals has been seen on the roadsides in many states. The strips of land next to roads had been home to a variety of trees and wildflowers throughout the northeastern US. But after the salesmen for chemical companies told the local governments that spraying was faster and easier than cutting, the result was dead, brown roadsides. When residents complained that their towns had become ugly for lack of pretty roadside flowers, the chemical company representatives laughed at them.

We must consider other reasons than just natural beauty, as important as it is. Of the 70 species of plants that typically grow on roadsides in the east, 65 are important to wildlife as food. Not only that, but these plants are the homes of wild bees, which humans depend on. Our food crops need bees to pollinate them in order to grow. When chemical spraying kills these plants, bees have nowhere to go. The cycle of life is broken once again.

We know herbicides don't always work the way we want them to. The goal of spraying roadsides is to kill tall plants that make driving unsafe. Selective spraying can more easily and safely achieve this goal, however. Another way to make sure taller plants like trees don't grow on roadsides is to plant bushes that keep trees out.

Herbicides are thought to be less poisonous than insecticides, but some have strange effects on animals. Both wild animals and cows have become attracted to plants sprayed with herbicides, even if they usually do not eat those plants. The herbicide somehow causes the plant to create sugar, making it attractive to many animals.

The herbicide 2,4-D can harm humans indirectly, as was seen when a number of "silo deaths" were reported. When 2,4-D is sprayed on some plants, such as corn or oats, it causes their nitrate levels to rise. These plants are stored in silos before being sent to stores. While inside the silo, the nitrates are changed into poisonous nitrogen oxide gas. Whoever opens the silo door then breathes in this gas and dies.

There is a better way to control unwanted plants than spraying them with herbicides. An example of this is the Klamath weed problem in California. Klamath weed, or St. John's Wort, as it is called in Europe, traveled with humans from the eastern US to the west. It is not native to the area and is poisonous to cows. In Europe, the weed is not

St. John's Wort

a problem because insects eat most of it. The US government brought some of these insects from Europe to help keep the Klamath weed under control. Studies showed that the program had been more successful than was hoped for. The weed was reduced to only 1 percent of its previous amount.

This shows that insects can be helpful in weed control. We just need to pay more attention to the types of insects that eat different types of plants.

7

Needless Havoc

As long as humans are trying to defeat nature, we will leave a depressing record of species destruction for future generations. This has already been seen in the near-extinction of buffalo in the West. Now a new kind of destruction is coming due to the use of sprays to get rid of insects. Let us look at some of these spray programs to see what has happened.

In 1959 the Michigan Department of Agriculture sprayed aldrin over 27,000 acres near Detroit. The target was the Japanese beetle. It had appeared in the US in 1916 and had been kept under control in the eastern states through natural methods.

Japanese beetle

For some reason, however, states like Michigan and Illinois thought the best way to deal with the beetle was to spray it with deadly chemicals. Planes carrying aldrin dumped the poison over fields, homes, and schools. The police asked local media to tell people it was safe. The spray came down like snow and gathered in piles on sidewalks and roofs.

Within a few days, people were finding dead birds everywhere. Other animals were also affected. Veterinarians began treating many sick cats, who were more affected than other animals because they often licked their paws. People who had watched the spraying outside complained of nausea, vomiting, fever, and coughing. The Health Commissioner for the area said that the bird deaths and human sickness must have been due to something else.

In Illinois a similar program to get rid of the Japanese beetle began in 1954. The spray used was dieldrin, which is 50 times as poisonous as DDT. Birds that ate the poisoned beetles and worms died in large numbers within two weeks. Many types of birds were almost wiped out. The birds that did survive became unable to produce eggs with live babies inside. Land animals like squirrels, muskrats, and rabbits were found dead in the sprayed area. Most farms that were sprayed had farm cats, 90% of which died in the first season of spraying. Larger mammals like sheep and cows were also poisoned, and some died.

muskrat

The program at some point changed from dieldrin to the even more dangerous aldrin, which is 100 to 300 times as poisonous as

DDT in tests on quail. In one town, all the robins, brown thrashers, and starlings were killed. And the result of all this killing? The treatment of more than 100,000 acres only stopped the beetle for a short time. It continues moving west.

brown thrasher

starling

Eastern states like Connecticut, New Jersey, Delaware, and Maryland had controlled the beetle using a bacterial disease that is harmless to all other life. So why didn't Michigan and Illinois use this more effective treatment instead? The answer we are given is 'the cost.'

We just have to wait a couple of years for natural bacteria to work. Research is being done to create the bacteria in an artificial way that will be faster and less expensive. Then perhaps the nightmare of these programs in Michigan and Illinois will end.

The events described above lead us to ask not only scientific questions but also moral ones. Can a society go to battle with nature without destroying itself? The poisons used to get rid of the Japanese beetle did not just affect beetles. They caused suffering to all life that they touched. If we cause this kind of suffering to a living creature, don't we become less human as a result?

8

And No Birds Sing

In towns across the United States, a strange silence now greets bird lovers on early spring mornings. In the past people looked forward to seeing the color and beauty of the birds returning after the long winter. Now everything has changed. Parents and teachers have to explain to their children where the birds have gone and why. The children know from their school lessons that it is not legal to kill birds. So how have these protected creatures been silenced?

To understand the reason, we must look at another living thing that is found in many towns in the East and Midwest—the American elm tree. A fungus disease has killed thousands of them. Some states have decided to spray the trees to get rid of the beetles that carry the fungus.

One such state was Michigan. After the first spraying on the campus of Michigan State University, robins started dying and no one knew why. The insecticide company had said their product would not harm birds. Dr. George Wallace, a professor at the university, reported that the campus was like a graveyard for robins in 1955, one year after the spraying began.

George Wallace

In other places, the robins were also dying. In Wisconsin, 86–88% of robins were killed by spraying. And not only birds, but all types of mammals that eat earthworms were affected.

Shrews and moles are part of the cycle that includes the earthworm. They eat the poisoned worm and if they don't die from poison, they pass it on to larger animals like hawks and owls who hunt them.

We can ask ourselves if we want birds or we want elm trees, but it is not as simple as that. The terrible tragedy is that spraying is killing the birds, but it is not saving the elm trees. After six years of spraying, 86 percent of elm trees died on one university campus. It was found that half of the dead trees had the fungus disease.

There are other solutions to fight this tree disease. Places like New York City use strict cutting and burning of all affected trees with great success. There are also ways to replant the trees to make them less likely to get the disease. And planting a variety of trees keeps the disease from spreading so quickly.

Eagles have also been dying, and it is likely

that pesticides are the cause. Records of young eagles were kept by a bird expert at Hawk Mountain in Pennsylvania. He found that from 1935 to 1939, 40 percent of the birds were eaglets. Then from 1955 to 1959, only 20 percent of the birds were eaglets. In one year, 1957, only one eaglet was found for every 32 adult birds.

Other places have recorded similar numbers. We may guess what is doing this to eagles from what is happening to other birds. Eagles mainly eat fish, and fish live in areas near spraying, like in the Chesapeake Bay area where DDT is used to kill salt marsh mosquitoes. As we saw with the grebes in Clear Lake, the poison builds up in the birds' bodies, and they are less and less able to lay eggs.

Birds are dying in Europe also. Chemically treated seeds are planted in many places in the UK. Before 1956, the chemical used was a fungicide which didn't hurt birds. Then dieldrin, aldrin, and heptachlor were added to kill insects in the soil. Reports of dead birds started coming in from all over England. In 1961 a special committee was formed in the House of Commons to talk about the problem. The government decided to ban seed treatment with dangerous chemicals. It also decided to require field testing in addition to laboratory testing on chemicals. This is important because no testing was being done on animals in the wild.

Who has the right to decide that we need a world without insects more than a world without beautiful, graceful birds in the sky?

Rivers of Death

Within the Atlantic Ocean are streams of fresh water that lead back to the coast of Canada. Salmon and other fish follow these streams to the rivers where they lay eggs. In the fall of 1953, salmon in the Miramichi River in New Brunswick, Canada, laid their eggs in waters near forests of spruce, balsam, hemlock, and pine trees. This had been the salmon's habit for many thousand years. The Miramichi was one of the best salmon streams in North America, but that year something changed.

During the late fall and winter, the salmon

laid eggs in small holes dug by the mother fish. In the spring the eggs hatched and the babies lived off the nutrients of the egg sac. Along with these newborn fish were salmon that had hatched the previous two years. These older fish had shiny scales and bright red spots. They needed to feed constantly and usually found plenty of insects in the stream.

But in the summer of 1954 a large spraying program began in order to get rid of a pest called the spruce budworm. It attacks evergreen trees in large numbers about every 35 years. The government decided to spray millions of acres there to save the paper industry, which relied on the trees.

Soon after the spraying in the northwest Miramichi area, many young salmon and brook trout were found dead. Birds also died, and the insect life in the river went quiet. Baby flies were all gone, and there was nothing for the youngest salmon to eat. None of the salmon born in the spring of 1954 survived, and only one in six of the 1953 salmon lived. One-third of the fish that hatched in 1952 were killed.

There were also big changes in the streams themselves. The insects that used to fill the streams were gone. It will be years before the insect population is built back up enough to give the salmon enough to eat. Even when the Canadians try to add insects to the river, the insects cannot survive repeated spraying.

There are ways to solve this problem that will save the forests and the fish too. We do not have to turn our waterways into rivers of death. There have been cases where a natural enemy of the budworm has kept it under control. It is important to understand that chemical spraying of forest insects is not the best or only way.

Fish are not the only water creatures to be harmed by insecticides. Our nation's estuaries, salt marshes, and other coastal waters receive the poisoned waters of rivers, and there is also direct spraying to control mosquitoes or other insects. An example from Florida shows the terrible result of spraying in salt marshes near the coastline. All the fish and crabs in the area were killed. One type of crab, the fiddler crab, has a unique place in the local ecosystem. It is a source of food for many animals, like birds and raccoons.

fiddler crab

Shrimp, oysters, and clams have also been affected by insecticide spraying. One scientist from the Bureau of Commercial Fisheries explained that oysters and clams may not die from pesticide poison, but they keep the poison in their organs. This does not sound good for humans, of course, since we eat all of these seafoods.

We don't know the full effects of the chemical run-off to rivers, marshes, and oceans. When will the public become aware of the facts and demand more research about this most important issue?

10

Spraying from the Skies

We now have such a large number of areas being sprayed from airplanes that one British ecologist called it a "rain of death." Of course, these chemicals come into contact with not only insects, but humans and non-humans as well. These chemicals are showered down indiscriminately on towns and cities, as well as forests and farms.

Two spraying programs from the late 1950s have caused doubts among local people. They were supposed to get rid of gypsy moths in the northeastern US and fire ants in the South, but both failed.

gypsy moth (larvae)

Controlling the gypsy moth, which came to the US from Europe in 1869, has worked fairly well in the northeast for almost a hundred years. The natural control used by the Agricultural Department involved importing enemies of the moth from Europe. Local spraying and quarantines had also helped.

However, in 1956 the same Agricultural Department decided to spray almost a million acres in Pennsylvania, New Jersey, Michigan, and New York. Its goal was not just control, but complete destruction of the gypsy moth. The following year three million acres were sprayed even though local residents and conservationists strongly opposed the idea.

A dairy farmer in New York asked that her land not be sprayed because she had milk cows. But her land was sprayed twice, and two days later the milk from her cows was tested. It had 14 parts per million of DDT. Local farmers couldn't sell their vegetables because they were burned and spotted.

In the end, nothing was gained because the gypsy moth came back in larger numbers than before the spraying had begun.

Killing the fire ant in the South was another of the Department of Agriculture's goals. The fire ant was annoying but not a serious problem. However, in 1957, there was a sudden and forceful public campaign against the fire ant, and 20,000,000 acres over nine states were sprayed.

In 1958 the serious effects of this program were seen. Deaths of wildlife like raccoons and birds, as well as chickens, cows and family pets were reported. Birds that live mostly on the ground, like quail and wild turkeys, were completely killed and 90 percent of songbirds that lived in the trees died. Animals that did survive gave birth to young who did not live very long.

Ways of getting rid of fire ants have been

known for years. They make their home in tall piles of dirt and sand, so they are easy to see in a large field. Spraying these holes is cheap, about 23 cents per acre. The Agricultural Department program cost $3.50 per acre.

In the end, the program was a failure, not only because of how many animal lives it took but also because there were more fire ants at the end of the program than there were at the beginning.

11

Poisonous Food

There are many more dangers to us than just the spraying of insecticides on farms and forests. In our daily lives there are many opportunities to have contact with chemicals that can, after many years, become harmful. But as regular citizens, we are not aware of the deadly products all around us.

The cheerful displays of insecticides in stores invite customers to buy these products without any understanding of their dangers. They can easily be reached on shelves by small children. And if one of these products were accidentally dropped, the chemical could splash on anyone nearby. One chemical that people commonly use in their homes to kill moths contains DDD, but the warning message on the product is written in very small print. A study was done to find out how many people read the small type on the labels of the insecticide products. Only 15 people out of 100 knew about the warnings.

Before going outside, we have many choices of insecticide to put on our skin to keep mosquitoes and other insects away. Some of these can melt paint or break down fabric. Can we not guess what they might do to our own skin?

A number of people in Florida died of parathion poisoning after using it in their garden. Finally, the Florida government limited its use to those who had a license. In most states, however, it has become even easier to use dangerous chemicals in gardens and on grass. One can buy a container of insecticide to put on a water hose, so watering the grass and spraying it with poison becomes one easy step.

In one case, a doctor who gardened in his free time used DDT and malathion weekly for a year. As he sprayed the chemicals with his water hose or by hand, sometimes his skin and clothes would become wet. After a year, he became ill and was hospitalized. It was found that he had 23 parts per million of DDT in his fat. He had serious nerve damage, lost weight, and was very tired. He could not continue with this medical practice.

One topic that is often debated is how much chemical residue there is on the food we eat. If anyone asks for food to be poison-free, they are called crazy. In this uncertain situation, what are the actual facts?

We know for sure that people who died before the DDT era (beginning around 1942) had no DDT in their bodies. The general population had 5.3 to 7.4 parts per million of DDT in their bodies between 1954 and 1956. This level has probably risen for the general population and, of course, people in the spraying professions have much higher levels.

The US Public Health Service tested meals from restaurants and institutions like schools, prisons, and hospitals. *Every meal that was tested contained DDT.* It was also found that cooked fruit served at a prison had 69.6 parts per million, and bread there had 100.9 parts per million of DDT!

The highest amounts of chlorinated hydrocarbons are found in meat because these chemicals break down in fat. Fruits and vegetables have lower levels, but they cannot be washed or cooked out. Milk should not have any insecticide in it, according to the rules of the Food and Drug Administration. However, the chemicals are found whenever tests are done. Butter and other dairy products have the highest levels.

To find food free from DDT and other chemicals, one has to go as far as the Arctic area of Alaska. All of the food tested there, including fish, beaver, moose, cranberries and rhubarb, had no sign of DDT. Only the Eskimos who had gone to the hospital in the big city for surgery had DDT in their fat.

If farmers closely follow the directions on the product label, there should be no higher level of residue than is allowed by the FDA. However, it is common for farmers to spray more than is recommended or to spray too close to harvest time.

There is also the chance of accidental poisoning. A large amount of green coffee beans were poisoned when they were shipped in the same container as insecticide products. Packaged foods sitting in warehouses are sprayed with DDT, which can get into the boxes and poison the food.

People may ask, "Doesn't the government protect us from all this?" The answer is, unfortunately, "Only in a limited way." The FDA has two main problems. First, it only inspects food that is shipped between states. Second, its staff is too small to handle all the work.

What is the solution, then? One is to use less dangerous chemicals like pyrethrins, rotenone, ryania, or ones that come from plants. Also, we should consider a non-chemical solution. We need to continue to research insect diseases, like bacteria that target specific insects. There are many other possible solutions to keep food safe. (See Chapter 17).

12

The Human Price

The wave of chemicals being used in recent decades is causing serious public health issues. Not long ago, we were afraid of diseases like smallpox and cholera, but now we are faced with a different kind of danger—one that we ourselves have created.

These new environmental health problems are caused by things like pesticides and other chemicals. It is frightening because their effects are sometimes unseen.

So where do pesticides fit into the picture of environmental disease? We have already seen that they are poisoning the soil, water, and food. They have the power to make our rivers fishless and our gardens and forests silent and birdless. Since we humans are part of nature, how can we escape this poison that is now everywhere in our world?

The major problem is not sudden illness and death from contact with large amounts of chemicals. For the general population, we should be more worried about the effects of small amounts of these poisons taken in over a long time. Though the danger is very real, humans usually ignore disasters that seem unclear or far in the future.

In nature, there are certain connected patterns, as we have seen. When we poison flies in a stream, the salmon die. When we poison gnats in a lake, the poison travels through the food chain and kills birds near the lake. The web of connections that causes this is called ecology.

There is also an ecology in our bodies. The

cause of a problem may seem unrelated because it happens far away from the effect. Even small changes that happen in molecules can cause widespread changes in all parts of our bodies. This is how the human body works. But we usually look at only the major problems and try to find one simple cause.

Someone may say, "I have used dieldrin sprays on the lawn many times, but I've never gotten sick. So, it hasn't hurt me." It's not that simple, though. Anyone who uses these chemicals is storing up dangerous materials in the fat of their body. If the body fat changes, the poison may affect the person quickly. In New Zealand, a man who was trying to lose weight suddenly had signs of poisoning. The dieldrin in the fat of the man's body became activated when he lost weight. This could also happen to someone who loses weight because of an illness.

One of the most important facts about

chlorinated hydrocarbon insecticides is their effect on the liver. The liver is the most extraordinary organ in the body. It not only helps digest fats, but it also helps digest all food. It builds proteins, stores vitamins, and performs many other functions. Without a properly functioning liver, the body would not be able to defend itself against poisons. The liver can even change the chemical malathion to make it less poisonous. But now, due to the constant intake of insecticides from our food, water, and air, our livers cannot protect us.

The liver-related diseases hepatitis and cirrhosis have been increasing since the 1950s. Although it is hard to prove this is caused by the increasing use of insecticides, common sense tells us that there is a connection. Even if chlorinated hydrocarbons are not the main cause, it doesn't make sense to use poisons that have been proven to damage the liver.

DDT directly affects the nervous system in different ways. Two scientists tested DDT on themselves to learn about its effects. They reported tiredness and aching arms and legs, as well as mental problems and joint pain. Another British scientist put DDT on his skin and reported some of the same symptoms, plus strong shaking, just like the birds that were poisoned by DDT. Even after a year, he had not fully recovered.

Why doesn't everyone who uses insecticide have the same symptoms? It is because of individual sensitivity. It's possible that women and young people are more easily affected than older men. Also, people who do very little exercise outside are more sensitive than those who work or exercise outside. Some doctors think that contact with chemicals actually produces sensitivity like allergies or infections.

Interactions between two chemicals or

between chemicals and other materials like medicine or food additives also affect individuals differently. It is hard to say how humans will react because we are not like animals in a laboratory that have only been in contact with one chemical at a time.

These chemicals also damage the nervous system and brain. Dieldrin can have delayed effects like memory loss, sleeplessness, nightmares, and mania. Lindane gets stored in the brain and liver and may have long-lasting effects on the nervous system. After a German greenhouse worker used parathion, he had mild poisoning symptoms, but became paralyzed several months later. In another case, three chemical plant workers were treated for insecticide poisoning and two recovered. One female chemist, however, developed paralysis in both legs. Even after two years, she was unable to walk.

Some mental diseases have been reported

as a result of organic phosphate poisoning. A hospital in Melbourne, Australia found 16 cases of people who worked with insecticides. Their symptoms were memory loss, schizophrenia, and depression. These conditions and many more are a heavy price to pay for the short-term killing of a few insects. But we will continue to pay that price as long as we use chemicals that are dangerous to the nervous system.

13

Through a Narrow Window

The biologist George Wald compared his narrowly focused scientific research to a small window. He said that when you are far away from a narrow window, you can only see a small slice of light. But as you get

George Wald

closer to the window, the view becomes much wider. The same can be said for the human body. We first look at single cells and all their activities. Then we open to a larger view of the effects of dangerous chemicals on them. None of the body's organs can work without the function of energy-creating oxidation. But the chemicals used to kill insects, small animals, and weeds can cause problems with it.

Cellular oxidation happens in every cell in the body. Cells burn fuel to make the energy life needs. All these billions of gently burning fires give us life. If they stop burning, plants cannot grow and human brains cannot think, according to chemist Eugene Rabinowitch.

Fugene Rabinowitch

This step-by-step process happens without end, like a wheel that never stops turning. Each step in this process is controlled by an enzyme that is designed to do one thing and nothing else. Energy is made, waste like CO_2 and H_2O is removed, and the fuel goes to the next stage. This process is one of the wonders of the living world. The fact that all this happens in very small places only adds to the miracle.

Mitochondria are small packages of enzymes arranged in a special way on the cell walls. They are the "powerhouses" where most energy production happens. Scientists use the term ATP (adenosine triphosphate) for the stage when mitochondria produce and release energy. ATP gives each type of cell the type of energy it needs.

The energy of ATP is linked to the oxidation process in cells. If the link is broken, the energy is still there, but it has no power. It is like a car in neutral. You can make the engine race when you push the gas, but there is no power to move the vehicle. So what can cause the link to break? Radiation, chemicals like phenols, 2,4-D, and DDT are all capable of breaking it.

Enzymes control the process of producing energy in each cell, and every time one enzyme is destroyed or weakened, the cycle of oxidation stops. It's like putting a stick into a moving wheel.

This stick in the wheel can be DDT, malathion, or any number of other chemicals. These can block the whole process of energy production and prevent cells from getting usable oxygen. When cells do not get enough oxygen, it causes serious problems.

Scientists have caused normal cells to become cancer cells by keeping oxygen from them. And experiments have shown that lack of oxygen can lead to undeveloped organs or other deformities in animals.

There are signs that these types of problems could increase in our children. In 1961 the Office of Vital Statistics began to keep records of deformities of babies. The office seems to think that future generations of children will have more defects due to radiation and possibly the reactions of chemicals on unborn babies.

Fewer births are another effect of lower ATP. Both eggs and sperm require ATP for energy, and if the wheels of ATP slow down, eggs stop growing and die. This has been seen in bird eggs, but there is no reason to think that this problem could not happen to humans also.

Genetic damage due to human-made chemicals is becoming a very real danger. We can see the similar nature of radiation and chemicals. A living cell can be damaged by radiation if its ability to divide is harmed, its chromosome structure is changed, or its genes suddenly mutate. Mutations can also cause changes in future generations.

Every one of these effects of radiation can also happen due to insecticides and herbicides. They could cause disease right away to the person using the chemicals, or they could cause damage to future generations.

It was only in 1927 that the effects of radiation

were discovered. Dr. H.J. Muller found that if he brought an organism in contact with X-rays, he could cause mutations that affected future generations of the organism. In the 1940s it was discovered that mustard gas could cause the same mutations in fruit flies. This was the first time a chemical mutagen had been found. But now many other chemicals have been added to the list that can change the genetic material of living things.

We should now watch the basic drama of life in a living cell to understand how chemicals can change the genetic structure.

Cells need to have the power to increase, and this happens through mitosis, or nuclear division. Important changes happen in a cell that is getting ready to divide. First, the chromosomes in the nucleus move and divide, making a pattern that looks like a long string, with genes attached to it like beads on a necklace. Then, each chromosome divides and half of each cell, along with its genes, goes to the daughter cells. This is how each new cell gets a complete set of chromosomes with all the genetic information saved in them. In this way, a species can create more members of the same species.

This process of division and sharing genetic information is the same in all types of life, from humans to trees. Up to now, nothing has been powerful enough to disrupt or change it. But in recent times, man-made radiation and chemicals have been introduced into the world.

We have only recently become able to study the effect of the environment on human chromosomes, and few people are aware that chemicals might affect us the same way that radiation does. But tests of insects and plants show the terrible possibilities of gene mutation.

Mosquitoes that have been sprayed with DDT for several generations become strange creatures that are part male and part female. Plants sprayed with phenols show damage to their chromosomes, and other mutations in genes that cannot be reversed. Plants sprayed with benzene hexachloride or lindane develop tumors on their roots. The herbicide 2,4-D also causes tumors in plants. Cell division slows down. These are the same effects that radiation has on plants.

Some scientists don't believe chemicals can get all the way to egg and sperm cells as radiation does. Though there have not been enough studies on humans, we do know that DDT has been found in the genetic material of birds and larger mammals.

British and French researchers found in 1959 that some diseases are caused by chromosome number problems. For example, having 47 instead of 46 chromosomes leads to being born with Down syndrome. Leukemia patients usually lack a part of a chromosome in some of their blood cells.

Much research is being done on chromosome problems around the world. Mental disability seems to come from the copying of only one part of chromosome, as if the chromosome were broken somewhere in the process of cell division.

This field is so new that most scientists focus on what chromosomes are connected to disease and disability rather than finding the cause. Of course, it's not reasonable to think that all chromosome damage is caused by just one thing, but we should not overlook the fact that the environment is now filled with chemicals that are powerful enough to affect chromosomes directly. Isn't this too high a price to pay for a beautiful potato or a mosquito-free patio?

We can reduce this risk to future generations, but we are not doing enough. Chemical makers are required to test their products for poison levels, but they are not required to test for the effect on genes. Therefore, the companies do not do such tests.

14

One in Every Four

Cancer began so long ago that its beginning has been lost, but it started in the natural environment. Some elements like ultraviolet radiation and arsenic in rocks could poison food and water supplies. Whatever life was on the earth at that time faced these dangers and some life died, while other life survived. Cancer-causing elements exist in nature, but they are rare, and life has become accustomed to them.

Humans have also developed cancer-causing chemicals called carcinogens. Some of these are very old, like soot from fireplaces. After the industrial era began, so many of these chemicals were used that humans could not adapt to them. Just as the human body changes slowly over time, it changes slowly when it faces new conditions, like the introduction of poisonous chemicals.

Though cancer has a long history, our awareness of its causes has happened slowly. In 1775, a doctor stated that cancer in the men who swept the chimneys of London was caused by the soot they were covered in every day. Other examples like this continued to be found over the centuries. Men who worked in copper and tin factories in Wales had skin cancer. By the end of the 19th century, about six carcinogens were found in industrial workplaces. But in the 20th century, not only people who work close to carcinogens are affected. The general population also has contact with them. This includes children who are not yet born.

The Office of Vital Statistics keeps track of diseases. It reported that cancerous growths, such as tumors, were the cause of 15 percent of the deaths in 1958, compared with only four percent in 1900. The American Cancer Society has estimated that cancer will be found in two out of three American families. We know from animal experiments that five or six pesticides can be called carcinogens.

The following example shows that it can take years for the government to control an unsafe situation with chemicals. In 1955, when mite and tick spray was introduced, the makers asked the government to allow a small residue on food, 1 part per million, for the first two years. During that time, more tests would be done to see if the chemical was really a carcinogen. This meant that humans, like animals in a laboratory, were being tested. It was found by 1957 that the insecticide was a carcinogen, but it took another year of legal processes to change the residue allowed from 1 part per million to zero.

Many other chemicals have been found to be carcinogens. DDT has caused liver tumors on animal tests. Two herbicides called IPC and CIPC have produced skin tumors in mice.

Regarding the newer insecticides and herbicides, not enough time has gone by to see their effects. Most tumors and other problems develop slowly, as the following example shows. In the early 1920s, women who painted watch dials with glowing radioactive paint sometimes touched the paintbrush to their lips to get it wet. By doing this, they were swallowing small amounts of radium from the paint. Some of these women got bone cancer fifteen or more years later.

One exception has been found to the long-term nature of cancer development. Leukemia showed up in survivors in Hiroshima only three years after the atomic bombing. The Office of Vital Statistics in the US has shown that the death rate from blood and lymph problems increased from 11.1 per 100,000 in 1950 to 14.1 per 100,000 in 1960. Doctors have reported that in almost all the cases of diseases in blood-forming organs, people had used poisonous chemicals.

One housewife wanted to get rid of the spiders in her house and sprayed them with DDT. She became sick right after spraying, but then felt better, so she sprayed the next month too. Again, she became sick and recovered. Because she did not relate her sickness to the spraying, she sprayed her house a third time. But then she had new symptoms and was told she had leukemia. She died very soon after the third spraying.

Two young cousins in Czechoslovakia worked in a farming cooperative where they carried sacks of insecticide. One of the boys developed leukemia and died nine days later. Within three months, the other boy showed symptoms of leukemia and also died.

A case in Sweden is familiar to those who know about the Japanese fishing boat the Lucky Dragon and its fisherman Kuboyama. A Swedish farmer, like Kuboyama, was a healthy man. One day the farmer used DDT and benzene hexachloride on his farm. As he sprayed, the wind blew the poisonous dust around him. He became sick that evening and went into the hospital one week after the spraying. After two and a half months, he died. The examination of his body showed that his bone marrow was completely gone.

Aikichi Kuboyama

Daigo Fukuryu Maru

How has the normal process of cell division changed into the uncontrolled spread of cancer? One German biochemist, Professor Otto Warburg, has explained how a normal cell can become cancerous.

Otto Warburg

Professor Warburg believes radiation or carcinogenic chemicals damage the respiration of normal cells, which keeps them from having enough energy. When the cells lose energy, they cannot make ATP. Instead, the cells change to a process of fermentation in order to survive. The cells can never get respiration back, but they continue to divide. Little by little, fermentation makes as much energy as respiration. This process may cause them to become cancer cells.

Warburg's explanation answers many questions about cancer. One is the length of time some cancers take to develop. In rats, cancer appears quickly because the fermentation rate is quick. In humans, the fermentation rate is slower, sometimes measured in decades.

Another answer that Warburg's findings have given us is about amounts of carcinogens necessary to cause cancer. Small doses taken again and again are more damaging than a large amount taken once. The large amount kills the cells immediately, while the repeated small amounts allow some cells to live and continue dividing by fermentation.

The final answer from Warburg has to do with the almost unbelievable fact that to treat cancer, we must use the same thing that causes cancer. Radiation and some chemicals can cause cancer but are also used to treat it. Cancer treatment kills the damaged cells completely so they cannot continue to spread to normal cells.

Many of the chlorinated hydrocarbons, the phenols, and some herbicides prevent oxidation and energy production in cells. This is how sleeping cancer cells may be created. These cells go undiscovered for a long time until they become fully cancerous. The fact that they became cancerous due to chemicals could be forgotten because it was so long ago.

The cells in the body that are most active in multiplying are the ones that help produce blood. Bone marrow is the main red blood cell producer, sending around 10 million new cells per second into the bloodstream. Benzene, a chemical often found in insecticides, gets into the bone marrow and stays there for as long as 20 months. This is one of the causes of leukemia. Leukemia is becoming more common in children. One scientist has said that this must mean the children had some type of cell mutation around the time of birth.

The chemical urethane has been shown to cause cancer in mice and their babies. It was proved that urethane went through the placenta of the pregnant mice to harm the babies. Dr. Hueper has warned that this could happen in humans. If a pregnant woman comes into contact with this chemical that is used in insecticides as well as medicine, clothing, and insulation, her unborn baby could develop tumors.

Another way that pesticides can cause cancer is more indirect than the explanations above. The chemicals in pesticides have been shown to damage the liver. They also reduce the supply of B vitamins, which are believed to slow or prevent the growth of cancer. When the liver doesn't work properly, the body's estrogen levels increase to unusually high levels. Too much estrogen has been found to cause tumors in test animals.

Humans come in contact with many different kinds of cancer-causing chemicals, including pesticides. Arsenic, for example, is found in everything from air pollution to food to cosmetics. None of these would be enough to cause disease by themselves, but over a period of time, they can combine and cause disease to develop.

The combination of DDT with other hydrocarbons, for example, could cause damage to liver cells. Hydrocarbons are found in paint removers, dry-cleaning materials, and anesthetics. Can there really be a "safe dose" of DDT?

Cancer sometimes needs two chemicals acting together to grow. One chemical prepares the cell, and the second chemical makes the cell diseased. Leukemia, for example, might be a two-step process. First, contact with radiation may damage the cell. Then contact with a chemical like urethane fully activates cancer development.

Water pollution from detergents is becoming a big concern for experts. Detergents by themselves are not carcinogenic, but they could cause cancer indirectly. They change tissues in the digestive areas so that dangerous chemicals are more easily taken in. In this world of changing conditions, the only "safe" dose of a carcinogen is zero.

When you discover that you live in a "sea of carcinogens," as one researcher put it, it is easy to give up. "Isn't it a hopeless situation?" is a common question. Another one is, "Isn't it better to find a cure for cancer than to get rid of all the cancer-causing materials in the world?"

Dr. Hueper believes that what we are facing today with cancer is similar to what people in the late 19th century faced with infectious diseases. Those illnesses, like tuberculosis and cholera, were controlled in two ways: prevention and cure. For example, when cholera was spreading through London more than a hundred years ago, a doctor found that many started in one area. All the residents of this area got their water from the same pump, so the doctor took off the pump handle. He did not have a magic pill to cure the disease, as important as that could be, but he slowed the spread of the infection by keeping people away from the cause of the cholera.

Today, we live in a world filled with cancer-producing elements. A battle with cancer that relies only on a cure, even if it could be found, will fail because the carcinogens are still out there. New victims will be made faster than the cure could work.

The solution to the cancer problem will not come through a sudden breakthrough. It will come one step at a time. We have a golden opportunity to prevent cancer at the same time that we work on a cure. It is not hopeless. It is actually more positive than the case of infectious disease. Those diseases were not caused by humans, but today's problems are man-made.

Therefore, humans can, if they want to, get rid of many of them.

There is a possibility of reducing the disease that takes 'one in every four people.' We should work hard to get rid of the carcinogens that affect our food, our water, and our atmosphere. Of course, we will continue to look for a cure. But for future generations, we must do as much as possible to prevent the problem of cancer.

15

Nature Fights Back

Up until now, we have risked a lot with chemical sprays but have failed to achieve the goal of insect control. The Dutch biologist C. J. Briejèr says that insects are amazing and that they can do the impossible. The "impossible" is now happening in two general ways. First, they are becoming resistant to chemicals. This will be discussed in the next chapter. Second, chemical spraying lowers the defenses that nature has built to control various species.

Chemical controls are self-defeating. Spraying may get rid of the target insect in the short term, but it also allows other, sometimes more harmful, insects to grow in large numbers. This happens because the sprays are tested only on a few species, not on the whole community of insects in their natural environment.

What we call the balance of nature is not an old idea that only existed in the simpler world of the past. Throughout time living things have had a complex system of relationships. Humans are one part of this balanced system. Sometimes the balance is in humans' favor and sometimes it is not, usually due to our own activities.

When spraying programs were created, two important facts were forgotten. First, within the balance of nature, insect numbers are controlled naturally. The weather, availability of food, and other species keep one type of insect from taking over. Second, species reproduce in large numbers if their natural enemies are taken away. An example of this is the Kaibab deer in Arizona. When the deer and the environment were in balance, the deer's predators, like wolves, puma, and coyotes

Kaibab deer (mule deer)

kept the deer population at correct levels. There was always enough food for the number of deer. But when people started killing the predators in order to "save the deer," the deer population increased greatly and food became hard to find. The deer had to go farther to get their food, damaging the environment in the process. More deer died of lack of food and disease than had been killed by their enemies.

We are mostly unaware of how natural enemies work in nature. We might see the mantis in the garden during the day, but we don't know how it hunts its prey dramatically at night. If we could see this drama, we might better understand the way nature controls life on its own.

There are many types of predators or insects that kill and eat other insects. Flying insects like yellow jackets and wasps eat insects like aphids and flies. Ladybugs are the best killers of aphids and other plant-eating insects.

Parasites are different from predators because they don't kill their enemies but use them to feed their young. In every field, forest, and garden, predators and parasites are at work. The dragonfly catches mosquitoes in the air with its basket-shaped legs. The dragonfly babies in the water below eat the water-based young of mosquitoes and other insects. This process continues throughout the days and nights in all kinds of weather. Even in winter, predators and parasites are waiting in trees and other protected places until it is warm again.

All these insects have been keeping nature's balance on our side. But we have started killing these friends. Over time we can expect an outbreak of disease-carrying and plant-destroying species of insects in amounts we have never seen before.

This is not a theory; it is already happening. For example, blackflies in Ontario are 17 times more abundant now than when spraying started. In England, a record outbreak of cabbage aphid happened after spraying with organic phosphorus chemicals.

Cabbage Aphids

The spider mite has become a worldwide problem because DDT spraying has killed all its enemies.

In 1956 the United States Forest Service sprayed 885,000 acres with DDT to kill the spruce budworm. The next summer there was a worse problem than the budworm. Many Douglas fir trees were turning brown and losing their needles because there was a record outbreak of spider mites in the area that was sprayed.

There are two reasons the spider mite population grows so much after spraying. First, their natural enemies, like the ladybug, are very sensitive to chemicals

Douglas fir

and die quickly. The second reason can be explained by the way the spider mite lives. These mites gather together in treetops and cover themselves with white webbing to stay hidden from their enemies. But the spraying causes these groups to leave their protected home and go out on their own to find food. Without natural enemies, they don't need to live in one place or spend energy to make the white webbing. Therefore, they can make more eggs, sometimes three times the number of eggs they could make with no chemical spraying.

What about insects that carry disease? On Nissan Island in the South Pacific, spraying was done during World War II, but stopped when the war ended. After that, many malaria-carrying mosquitoes took over the island because all of their predators had been killed.

It has taken a long time for us to see the problems described above. Why is this? In 1960, it was reported that only 2 percent of all economic entomologists in the US were working in the field of biological controls. That means that most of the other 98 percent had jobs in the chemical industry. The chemical companies give a lot of money to universities to do research on insecticides.

One result of this situation is that most entomologists become supporters of the chemical companies and will not say anything bad about the effects of chemical spraying. They do not want to lose their nice jobs with high salaries.

An entomologist working in the apple orchards of Nova Scotia, Canada, is an example of an expert who did not follow most scientists down the path of DDT spraying. After DDT caused problem after problem, Dr. A. D. Pickett made a program that uses natural controls and only a little insecticide. He found that the timing of the spraying is important. Using a small amount of insecticide before the apple flowers turn pink, an important predator of the unwanted insect is kept alive because it is still in the egg stage at the time of spraying and is not affected by the spray. Farmers who follow Dr. Pickett's program are getting the same amount of fruit as the ones who are using insecticides. And they are paying much less, 10 to 20 percent of what other farmers pay. We must admit that, in many cases, nature can find ways to limit populations in a more economical way than humans can.

The Rumblings of
an Avalanche

If Darwin could see the insect world today, he would be excited to see that his theories of 'survival of the fittest' are working as he said they would. Because of the deadly chemicals being used on insects, the weaker ones are being killed, while the stronger ones live and make more babies, ensuring their survival.

In the world before DDT, there were some insects that survived chemical spraying. But after DDT was created, resistance became much more of a problem. The only people who seem concerned with this situation are the scientists who study insects carrying disease. The list of disease-carrying insects is long, and includes body lice, rat fleas, tsetse flies, ticks, and many others.

Insecticides were first used for medical purposes in Italy during World War II, when people were dusted with DDT to prevent typhus and malaria. But three years later, both houseflies and mosquitoes were showing resistance to the DDT.

DDT was widely used to control body lice DDT in Italy, Japan, and Korea in the 1940s. The first sign of trouble was when a typhus outbreak was not controlled in Spain in 1948. However, countries still used DDT powder to control lice, and the lice developed resistance in Korea, Japan, Syria, Jordan, and many other countries by 1957.

Ticks are a problem for both humans and dogs. Even though they are semi-tropical insects, they have been found in heated buildings in the northern US. In 1959, people living near Central Park in New York City were faced with a tick outbreak. After walking their dogs in the park, they came home, and the ticks laid eggs. These insects were resistant to DDT and chlordane and were almost impossible to get rid of.

Insects that eat crops are also developing resistance to chemical sprays. The codling moth is found in almost all of the world's apple-growing areas and is now resistant to DDT.

codling moth (larvae)

The chemical industry does not, understandably, want to admit this fact. But the problem is not going away, and it causes economic loss, along with crop damage and human disease. When companies invest in potentially successful chemicals, they may lose a lot of money if the chemical doesn't work due to insect resistance. Insects will likely continue to stay ahead of humans in this war of chemicals against nature.

How do insects become resistant to these powerful chemicals? There are many answers, and most of them are not completely understood. Even when bedbugs in Taiwan had DDT powder on their legs, they seemed unaffected. Some were even filled with DDT and lived for a month, long enough to lay eggs and for their babies to survive.

Some flies that show resistance to DDT have an enzyme that enables them to change DDT to the less poisonous DDE. Other flies change their behavior to avoid surfaces with the most DDT on them. Generally, resistance takes a couple of years to develop, but sometimes it can come within a season or less.

Some people may ask, can't humans develop the same resistance to the chemicals that insects have? They could, but it would take hundreds or thousands of years. It takes many generations for humans to pass survival factors to their children. For insects that can happen in days or weeks.

The Department of Agriculture's Yearbook for 1952 says the answer to insect resistance is to spray more often in greater quantities. The Yearbook does not say what will happen when the earth is left not only insect-free but also life-free after the last available chemical is tried.

Life is a miracle beyond anything we can understand. We should honor and respect it. Using weapons like insecticides to control life shows what little knowledge we have. We must be humble, rather than egotistical.

The Other Road

Robert Frost

In Robert Frost's famous poem, he asks us to choose between the road we are on and the 'road less traveled.' This is where we find ourselves now: looking at two ways to go. The road we've been on is easy. But it ends in disaster. The 'less-traveled road,' on the other hand, is the only one by which we can save our earth. Now that we know what is happening, we should look around us at what other options are open to us.

There are many alternatives to chemical

control of insects. Some are being used with success already, and others are in the testing stage. One of these new ideas is to sterilize the male of an insect species in order to destroy it.

Edward Knipling

Dr. Edward Knipling of the US Department of Agriculture wanted to try sterilization in a small setting. He chose to sterilize the screw-worm fly, which eats the cow meat. Dr. Knipling went to an island in the Caribbean to test his idea. He wanted to release sterilized flies so that the eggs produced would be unable to hatch into new flies. Just seven weeks after the flies were dropped by airplane, the only eggs they found on the island were infertile. Then the eggs disappeared completely because there were no male flies left that could fertilize them. This marked an important success for creativity, research, and persistence.

Scientists are now trying to copy the same idea and use it on other insects. Dr. Knipling used radiation to sterilize his flies, but this method doesn't work well on a large scale. Using chemicals to sterilize is now being tested in several places. In Florida, the Department of Agriculture is doing trials on houseflies. Chemicals that sterilize are combined with food that flies like. This combination is applied to areas where flies live, and within a short period of time, all the flies can be killed. Dr. Knipling has said that this method "might easily outdo some of the best-known insecticides."

Of course, using chemicals to sterilize insects needs to be done with safety in mind. Chemicals should not be sprayed from the air without research into the effects on all life below. We could be in a worse situation than we are now with chemical poisons.

Another alternative to insecticides is using

the insects' own weapons against them. These weapons include venom, repellents, and attractants. One example is the gypsy moth. The female moth is too large to fly, so she lives near the ground and attracts the male moth by releasing a scent. Scientists have been able to copy the scent using artificial ingredients and release it from planes. The idea is to confuse the male moth so that he cannot find the real female.

melon fly

In another case, the male melon fly is attracted to a certain smell. Scientists have combined the scent with poison and sprayed it on light cardboard. They dropped these pieces of board all over an island chain south of Japan. One year later, it was estimated that 99% of the fly population was gone. The other good points of this method are that the poison on the board is not likely to be eaten by other animals and it disappears quickly, so it will not poison the soil or water.

What possible use could be made of sounds which insects react to? An interesting experiment is also being done on male mosquitoes. A recording of females is played to attract the males. When the males fly close to the sound, they are killed with an electric charge. Such experiments are just the first steps toward a completely new way of controlling insects.

There is also another way to get rid of unwanted insects. A type of bacteria was discovered in Germany in 1911. It quickly kills the target insect, in this case the flour moth, with poison instead of disease. This means that the flour moth stops eating the plant soon after the poi-

flour moth

root borer (Rhabdoscelus obscurus)

sonous bacteria are taken in. A very hopeful test is being done in Panama, where the root borer causes great damage to banana trees. Using this insecticide instead of dieldrin kills the borers quickly but keeps other nearby insects and animals safe.

Even though biological control is cheaper and safer than insecticides, it does not have enough support. Only one of the U.S. states, California, has a formal program in biological control. Some European countries have taken biological control the farthest. For example, a professor in Germany has used a predator, the red ant, to get rid of unwanted insects in large parts of the German forest. His idea is being used in Italy and other countries.

red ant (Formica rufa)

These new and creative ideas all have a common theme: the awareness that we are dealing with life in all its systems. Only by considering these life forces will we be able to achieve a balance between ourselves and the insect populations around us. The use of poisons does not consider these systems at all. Chemicals are a low-level weapon, like a caveman's club, that harms the delicate fabric of life.

Trying to control nature is an egotistical idea that shows that we believe nature exists for our convenience. We have a very old way of looking at insect control, and now this old way is using modern weapons which not only destroy insects, but the earth itself.

Word List

・本文で使われている全ての語を掲載しています（LEVEL 1、2）。ただし、LEVEL 3 以上は、中学校レベルの語を含みません。

・語形が規則変化する語の見出しは原形で示しています。不規則変化語は本文中で使われている形になっています。

・一般的な意味を紹介していますので、一部の語で本文で実際に使われている品詞や意味と合っていないことがあります。

・品詞は以下のように示しています。

名 名詞	代 代名詞	形 形容詞	副 副詞	動 動詞	助 助動詞
前 前置詞	接 接続詞	間 間投詞	冠 冠詞	略 略語	俗 俗語
頭 接頭語	尾 接尾語	記 記号	関 関係代名詞		

A

☐ **A. D. Pickett** アリソン・デフォレスト・ピケット（Allison Deforest Pickett）《カナダの昆虫学者。DDT のような広範囲の殺虫剤が台頭していた時期に、生物的防除と標的化された殺虫剤の使用を推進した。1900–1991》

☐ **ability** 名 ①できること、（〜する）能力 ②才能

☐ **about** 熟 be worried about（〜のことで）心配している、〜が気になる［かかる］ come about 起こる What about 〜? 〜はどうですか。 worry about 〜のことを心配する

☐ **absorb** 動 ①吸収する ②《be -ed in 〜》〜に夢中である

☐ **abundant** 形 豊富な、たくさんの

☐ **accidental** 形 偶然の、不慮の

☐ **accidentally** 副 偶然に、誤って

☐ **according to** 〜によれば［よると］

☐ **accustom to** 〜に慣れさせる

☐ **achieve** 動 成し遂げる、達成する、成功を収める

☐ **aching** 形 （ズキズキと）痛む、うずく

☐ **acre** 名 エーカー《面積の単位。約 4,046.7 平方メートル》

☐ **act** 動 ①行動する ②機能する ③演じる

☐ **activate** 動 ①動かす、作動させる ②活性化する、盛んにする

☐ **activated** 形 活性化した

☐ **active** 形 ①活動的な ②積極的な ③活動［作動］中の

☐ **activity** 名 活動、活気

☐ **actual** 形 実際の、現実の

☐ **actually** 副 実際に、本当に、実は

☐ **adapt** 動 ①適応する［させる］ ②脚色する、編曲する、翻案する

☐ **add** 動 ①加える、足す ②足し算をする ③言い添える

☐ **addition** 名 ①付加、追加、添加 ②足し算 in addition 加えて、さらに

☐ **additive** 名 添加物、添加剤《着色料や香料、防腐剤など、食品やガソリンなどに添加される物質のこと》

☐ **adenosine triphosphate** アデノシン三リン酸（ATP）《生物学的なエネルギーの基本的な分子であり、細胞内でエネルギーを蓄積・転送・利用するための主要な分子》

☐ **adjust** 動 ①適応する［させる］、慣

れる ②調整する ③（意見の食い違い・論争などを）解決する, 調停する ④（間違いなどを）訂正する

□ **adjusted** 形 調整される

□ **administration** 名 管理, 統治, 政権

□ **admit** 動 認める, 許可する, 入れる

□ **adult** 名 大人, 成人 形 大人の, 成人した

□ **advertise** 動 ①広告する, 宣伝する ②告知する

□ **advice** 名 忠告, 助言, 意見

□ **affect** 動 ①影響する ②（病気などが）おかす

□ **afraid of** 《be –》～を恐れる, ～を怖がる

□ **after that** その後

□ **again and again** 何度も繰り返して

□ **agent** 名 ①代理人 ②代表者

□ **ago** 熟 long ago ずっと前に, 昔

□ **agricultural** 形 農業の, 農事の

□ **Agricultural Department** 農務省

□ **agriculture** 名 農業, 農耕

□ **ahead of** ～より先［前］に, ～に先んじて

□ **air pollution** 大気汚染

□ **airplane** 名 飛行機

□ **Alabama** 名 アラバマ州

□ **Alaska** 名 アラスカ州

□ **Albert Schweitzer** アルベルト・シュヴァイツァー《ドイツ生まれのフランスの哲学者, 神学者, 医師, 音楽家。1875–1965》

□ **aldrin** 名 アルドリン《有機塩素系の農薬で, 特に害虫駆除に用いられた》

□ **algae** 名 藻（類）《複》

□ **all kinds of** さまざまな, あらゆる種類の

□ **all over** ～中で, 全体に亘って, ～の至る所で

□ **all the way** ずっと, はるばる, いろいろと

□ **allergy** 名 アレルギー

□ **allow** 動 ①許す, 《– … to ～》…が～するのを可能にする, …に～させておく ②与える

□ **alternative** 名 2つのうちの1つ, 代替え手段, 代替案

□ **although** 接 ～だけれども, ～にもかかわらず, たとえ～でも

□ **always** 熟 not always 必ずしも～であるとは限らない

□ **amazing** 形 驚くべき, 見事な

□ **America** 名 アメリカ《国名・大陸》

□ **American** 形 アメリカ（人）の 名 アメリカ人

□ **American Cancer Society** 米国がん協会

□ **American elm** アメリカニレ

□ **amitrol** 名 アミトロール《非選択的な除草剤の一種として, 農地や産業用地, 鉄道の線路などでの雑草の管理に利用される》

□ **amount** 名 量

□ **anesthetics** 名 麻酔学

□ **annoying** 形 人を悩ます, いらいらさせる

□ **ant** 名 アリ

□ **antelope** 名 レイヨウ, アンテロープ《枝分かれしない角を持つウシ科の偶蹄類の総称》

□ **any** 熟 than any other ほかのどの～よりも

□ **anyone** 代 ①《疑問文・条件節で》誰か ②《否定文で》誰も（～ない）③《肯定文で》誰でも

□ **aphid** 名 アブラムシ

□ **appear** 動 ①現れる, 見えてくる ②（～のように）見える, ～らしい

□ **apple-growing** 形 リンゴ栽培の

□ **apply** 動①申し込む, 志願する ②あてはまる ③適用する

□ **approve** 動賛成する, 承認する

□ **Arctic** 形北極の 名《the –》北極地方

□ **Arizona** 名アリゾナ州

□ **around** 熟 look around まわりを見回す

□ **arranged** 形配列[配置]された

□ **arsenic** 名ヒ素《元素記号がAsで, 原子番号が33の元素。自然界には主に硫化鉱石として存在し, 半導体や殺虫剤, 木材防腐剤などに利用される》

□ **artificial** 形人工的な

□ **as** 熟 as a result その結果 (として) as a result of ～の結果 (として) as ～ as one can できる限り～ as ～ as possible できるだけ～ as far as ～と同じくらい遠く, ～まで, ～する限り (では) as if あたかも～のように, まるで～みたいに as long as ～する以上は, ～である限りは, ～もの長い間 as much as ～と同じだけ as well なお, その上, 同様に as well as ～と同様に just as (ちょうど)～であろうとおり such as たとえば～, ～のような such ～ as … …のような～ the same ～ as … …と同じ (ような) ～ times as … as A A～の～倍の…

□ **ask ～ if** ～かどうか尋ねる

□ **aspirin** 名アスピリン

□ **astonishing** 形驚くべき

□ **at** 熟 at a time 一度に at least 少なくとも at that time その時 at the end of ～の終わりに at the rate of ～ per year 年～の割合で at the time そのころ, 当時は at work 働いて, 仕事中で, (機械が) 稼動中で

□ **Atlantic Ocean** 大西洋

□ **atmosphere** 名①大気, 空気 ②雰囲気

□ **atom** 名原子

□ **atomic** 形①原子[原子力・原子力爆弾]の[に関する] ②極小の ③原子状の

□ **atomic bombing** 原爆投下

□ **ATP (adenosine triphosphate)** 略アデノシン三リン酸《生物学的なエネルギーの基本的な分子であり, 細胞内でエネルギーを蓄積・転送・利用するための主要な分子》

□ **attached** 形ついている, 結びついた

□ **attack** 動①襲う, 攻める ②非難する ③(病気が) おかす 名①攻撃, 非難 ②発作, 発病

□ **attention** 名①注意, 集中 ②配慮, 手当て, 世話

□ **attract** 動①引きつける, 引く ②魅力がある, 魅了する

□ **attractant** 名誘引物質《生物が他の生物に対して好奇心や興味を持ちやすいように作られた物質のこと》

□ **attractive** 形魅力的な, あいきょうのある

□ **Australia** 名オーストラリア《国名》

□ **availability** 名①利用できること, 入手できるもの ②有益, 有用性

□ **available** 形利用[使用・入手]できる, 得られる

□ **avalanche** 名雪崩

□ **average** 名平均 (値), 並み

□ **avoid** 動避ける, (～を) しないようにする

□ **aware** 形①気がついて, 知って ②(～の) 認識のある be aware of ～に気がついている

□ **awareness** 名認識, 自覚, 意識性, 気づいていること

□ **away** 熟 far away 遠く離れて get washed away 押し流される go away 立ち去る right away すぐに take away ①連れ去る ②取り上げる, 奪い去る ③取り除く wash away 押し流す

B

- ☐ **B vitamins** 水溶性のビタミンB群の総称
- ☐ **baby** 熟 have a baby 赤ちゃんを産む
- ☐ **back** 熟 come back 戻る fight back 反撃に転じる, 応戦する get ~ back ~を取り返す[戻す]
- ☐ **bacteria** 名バクテリア, 細菌
- ☐ **bacterial** 形細菌の
- ☐ **bacterial disease** 細菌性疾患, 細菌性の病気
- ☐ **balance** 名均衡, 平均, 落ち着き
- ☐ **balanced** 形バランス[釣り合い・均衡]の取れた
- ☐ **balsam** 名バルサムモミ
- ☐ **ban** 名禁止, 禁制 動禁止する
- ☐ **banana** 名バナナ
- ☐ **bare** 形裸の, むき出しの
- ☐ **basic** 形基礎の, 基本の
- ☐ **basket-shaped** 形籠形の
- ☐ **battle** 名戦闘, 戦い
- ☐ **bay** 名湾, 入り江
- ☐ **bead** 名《-s》ビーズ[のネックレス]
- ☐ **bean** 名豆
- ☐ **bear** 名熊
- ☐ **beauty** 名①美, 美しい人[物] ②《the –》美点
- ☐ **beaver** 名ビーバー
- ☐ **because of** ~のために, ~の理由で
- ☐ **bedbug** 名トコジラミ
- ☐ **bee** 名ミツバチ
- ☐ **beekeeping** 名養蜂
- ☐ **beet** 名ビート, サトウダイコン
- ☐ **beetle** 名甲虫, カブトムシ
- ☐ **beginning** 名初め, 始まり
- ☐ **behavior** 名振る舞い, 態度, 行動
- ☐ **being** 動 be (~である) の現在分詞

名存在, 生命, 人間 **human being** 人, 人間
- ☐ **belong to** ~に属する, ~のものである
- ☐ **below** 前①~より下に ②~以下の, ~より劣る 副下に[へ]
- ☐ **benefit** 名利益, 恩恵
- ☐ **benzene** 名ベンゼン《有機化合物であり, 分子式がC_6H_6で表される環状の炭化水素。化学工業において非常に重要な原料。有機合成の出発物質として, プラスチック, 合成ゴム, 染料, 医薬品, 農薬などの製造に使われる》
- ☐ **benzene hexachloride** ベンゼンヘキサクロライド《かつて殺虫剤として広く使用されていた有機塩素系の化学物質》
- ☐ **berry** 名ベリー《イチゴ, スグリなどの小果実》
- ☐ **best-known** 形最もよく知られた
- ☐ **better** 熟 feel better 気分がよくなる
- ☐ **beyond** 前~を越えて, ~の向こうに 副向こうに
- ☐ **billion** 形10億の, ばく大な, 無数の 名10億
- ☐ **biochemist** 名生化学者
- ☐ **biocide** 名殺生物剤
- ☐ **biological** 形生物学(上)の, 生物学的な **biological control** 生物(学)的防除[駆除・コントロール]
- ☐ **biologist** 名生物学者
- ☐ **birdless** 形鳥のいない
- ☐ **birth** 名①出産, 誕生 ②生まれ, 起源, (よい)家柄 **give birth to** ~を生む
- ☐ **blackfly** 名ブユ
- ☐ **blew** 動 blow (吹く) の過去
- ☐ **blood** 名血, 血液
- ☐ **blood-forming organ** 造血臓器

☐ **bloodstream** 名 血流

☐ **board** 名 板

☐ **body lice** ヒトジラミ

☐ **bombing** 名 爆撃, 爆破

☐ **bond** 動 接着する [させる], 結合する

☐ **bone** 名 ①骨,《-s》骨格 ②《-s》要点, 骨組み 動 (魚・肉)の骨をとる

☐ **bone cancer** 骨肉腫

☐ **bone marrow** 骨髄

☐ **booming** 形 好景気の, 活況の

☐ **borer** 名 木や果実に穴を開ける虫, 穿孔(性)動物

☐ **both A and B** AもBも

☐ **brain** 名 脳

☐ **breakthrough** 名 突破, 打開, ブレークスルー

☐ **breast milk** 母乳

☐ **breathe** 動 ①呼吸する ②ひと息つく, 休息する

☐ **British** 形 ①英国人の ②イギリス英語の 名 英国人

☐ **brook** 名 小川

☐ **brook trout** カワマス

☐ **brown thrasher** チャイロツグミモドキ

☐ **budworm** 名 花や針葉樹の芽や葉を食べるイラクサガ科のガの幼虫のこと

☐ **buffalo** 名 野牛, バッファロー

☐ **building** 名 建物, 建造物, ビルディング

☐ **building block** 構成要素, 基本単位

☐ **bureau** 名 ①案内所, 事務所 ②局, 部

☐ **Bureau of Commercial Fisheries** 商業漁業局

☐ **burning** 動 burn (燃える)の現在分詞 形 燃えている

☐ **bush** 名 低木の茂み

☐ **butter** 名 バター

☐ **by** 熟 **by oneself** 一人で, 自分だけで, 独力で **go by** (時が) 過ぎる, 経過する **little by little** 少しずつ

C

☐ **C. J. Briejèr** コルネリス・ヤン・ブリエイェ (Cornelis Jan Briejèr)《オランダの農学者で, DDTが鳥類に与える影響について研究した。ジョージ・ウォレスと共同で, DDTが鳥類の卵殻の薄化や繁殖の減少を引き起こすことを発見した。1901–1986》

☐ **cabbage aphid** ダイコンアブラムシ

☐ **calculate** 動 ①計算する, 算出する ②見積もる, 予想する

☐ **California** 名 カリフォルニア《米国の州》

☐ **California Department of Public Health** カリフォルニア州公衆衛生局

☐ **calm** 動 静まる, 静める

☐ **campaign** 名 ①キャンペーン (活動, 運動) ②政治運動, 選挙運動

☐ **campus** 名 キャンパス, (大学などの) 構内

☐ **can** 熟 **as ~ as one can** できる限り ~ **can hardly** とても~できない

☐ **Canada** 名 カナダ《国名》

☐ **Canadian** 形 カナダ(人)の 名 カナダ人

☐ **cancer** 名 がん **bone cancer** 骨肉腫

☐ **cancer cell** がん細胞

☐ **cancer-causing** 形 発がん性の(ある), がんを誘発する

☐ **cancerous** 形 がん性の

☐ **cancer-producing** 形 がんを生じる

☐ **capable** 形 ①《be – of ~ [~ing]》

Word List

～の能力[資質]がある ②有能な

承知しました

□ **carbohydrate** 图炭水化物, 糖質《炭素, 水素, 酸素の原子からなる有機化合物で, 生物の主要な構成要素とエネルギー源の一つ》

□ **carbon** 图炭素

□ **carbon tetrachloride** 四塩化炭素《四つの塩素原子が炭素原子に結合した無機化合物で, 有機溶媒として以前広く使用されていた》

□ **carcinogen** 图発がん(性)物質

□ **carcinogenic** 形発がん性の(ある)

□ **cardboard** 图ボール紙, 厚紙

□ **careless** 形不注意な, うかつな

□ **Caribbean** 图カリブ海

□ **carrot** 图ニンジン

□ **case** 熟in the case of ～の場合は

□ **cattle** 图畜牛, 家畜

□ **caveman** 图(石器時代の男性の)穴居人

□ **cell** 图細胞 cancer cell がん細胞 red blood cell 赤血球

□ **cell division** 細胞分裂

□ **cell mutation** 細胞突然変異

□ **cell wall** 細胞壁

□ **cellular** 形細胞状の

□ **cellular oxidation** 細胞酸化《細胞内で酸素が使用されるプロセスを指す, 生物学や生化学の文脈で使われる用語。別名, 細胞呼吸》

□ **cent** 图セント《米国などの通貨単位。1ドルの100分の1》

□ **central** 形中央の, 主要な

□ **Central Park** セントラル・パーク《米ニューヨーク市マンハッタン区の中心にある市所有の公園》

□ **certain** 形①確実な, 必ず～する ②(人が)確信した ③ある ④いくらかの

□ **certainly** 副①確かに, 必ず ② 《返答に用いて》もちろん, そのとおり,

□ **chain of** 一連の～, ～の連鎖

□ **chapter** 图(書物の)章

□ **charge** 图電荷 electric charge 電荷

□ **Charles Darwin** チャールズ・ダーウィン《イギリスの自然科学者であり, 進化論の提唱者。種の進化に関する理論を提唱し, その著書『種の起源』(On the Origin of Species)で進化に関する概念を広めた。1809–1882》

□ **checkerboard** 图チェッカー盤, 市松[格子縞]模様のもの

□ **cheerful** 形上機嫌の, 元気のよい, (人を)気持ちよくさせる

□ **chemical** 形化学の, 化学的な 图化学製品[薬品]

□ **chemical run-off** 薬品流出

□ **chemically** 形化学的に

□ **chemist** 图化学者

□ **Chesapeake Bay** チェサピーク湾

□ **chick** 图ひよこ, ひな鳥

□ **chimney** 图煙突(状のもの)

□ **chlordane** 图クロルダン《有機塩素系の農薬で, 害虫駆除などに広く使用されていた》

□ **chloride** 图塩化物《塩化ナトリウムや塩化水素など, 塩素が他の元素や原子団と結合してできる化合物のこと》

□ **chlorinated hydrocarbon** 塩素化炭化水素《炭素(C)と水素(H)から構成される炭化水素に, 塩素(Cl)が結合した化合物》

□ **chlorine** 图塩素《原子番号17の元素で, 元素記号はCl。常温常圧では特有の臭いを有する黄緑色の気体で, 強い漂白・殺菌作用を持つ》

□ **chloroform** 图クロロホルム《化学的には$CHCl_3$と表される有機化合物。かつては麻酔薬として使用されていた》

129

- □ **choice** 名選択（の範囲・自由），選ばれた人［物］
- □ **cholera** 名コレラ
- □ **chromosome** 名染色体
- □ **chrysanthemum** 名菊
- □ **CIPC** 名クロロイソプロピルカルバミン酸エステル《IPCのクロロ誘導体で，IPCよりも土壌吸着性が高く，雑草の発芽を抑制する効果がある》
- □ **circle** 名①円，円周，輪 ②循環，軌道
- □ **cirrhosis** 名肝硬変
- □ **citizen** 名①市民，国民 ②住民，民間人
- □ **clam** 名ハマグリ，アサリ《二枚貝》
- □ **cleaning** 名掃除，クリーニング，洗濯
- □ **clear** 形①はっきりした，明白な ②澄んだ
- □ **Clear Lake** クリア・レイク《アメリカのカリフォルニア州にある湖の名》
- □ **climate** 名気候，風土，環境
- □ **close to** 《be－》～に近い
- □ **close to death** 死にかけである
- □ **closed** 形閉じた，閉鎖した
- □ **closely** 副①密接に ②念入りに，詳しく ③ぴったりと
- □ **clothing** 名衣類，衣料品
- □ **club** 名こん棒
- □ **CO₂** 名二酸化炭素（の分子式）
- □ **coast** 名海岸，沿岸
- □ **coastal** 形沿岸の，海岸線に沿った
- □ **coastline** 名海岸線
- □ **cockroach** 名ゴキブリ
- □ **codling moth** コドリンガ
- □ **Colorado** 名コロラド州
- □ **combination** 名結合（状態，行為）
- □ **combine** 動結合する［させる］

- □ **come** 熟come about 起こる come back 戻る come down 下りて来る come in やってくる come in contact with ～と接触する，～に出くわす come in ～ from ～から来る come into contact with ～と接触する，～に出くわす come through 通り抜ける，成功する，期待に沿う
- □ **commercial** 形商業の，営利的な
- □ **commissioner** 名委員，コミッショナー
- □ **committee** 名評議会，委員（会），受託人
- □ **common sense** 良識，常識
- □ **commonly** 副一般に，通例
- □ **commons** 熟House of Commons 庶民院，下院
- □ **community** 名①団体，共同社会，地域社会 ②《the－》社会（一般），世間
- □ **compare** 動①比較する，対照する ②たとえる
- □ **compartment** 名区画，仕切り
- □ **complain** 動①不平［苦情］を言う，ぶつぶつ言う ②（病状などを）訴える
- □ **complete** 形完全な，まったくの，完成した
- □ **completely** 副完全に，すっかり
- □ **complex** 形入り組んだ，複雑な，複合の
- □ **compound** 名合成物，化合物，複合物
- □ **concern** 名①関心事 ②関心，心配 ③関係，重要性
- □ **concerned** 形①関係している，当事者の ②心配そうな，気にしている
- □ **condition** 名①（健康）状態，境遇 ②《-s》状況，様子 ③条件
- □ **confuse** 動混同する，困惑させる，混乱させる

Word List

☐ **Congress** 名(米国などの)国会, 議会

☐ **connect** 動つながる, つなぐ, 関係づける

☐ **connected** 形結合した, 関係のある

☐ **Connecticut** 名コネティカット州

☐ **connection** 名①つながり, 関係 ②縁故

☐ **conservationist** 名自然保護活動家

☐ **consider** 動①考慮する, 〜しようと思う ②(〜と)みなす ③気にかける, 思いやる

☐ **constant** 形絶えない, 一定の, 不変の

☐ **constantly** 副絶えず, いつも, 絶え間なく

☐ **contact** 熟come in [into] contact with 〜と接触する, 〜に出くわす

☐ **contain** 動①含む, 入っている ②(感情などを)抑える

☐ **container** 名①容器, 入れ物 ②(輸送用)コンテナ

☐ **continuous** 形連続的な, 継続する, 絶え間ない

☐ **control** 動①管理[支配]する ②抑制する, コントロールする 名①管理, 支配(力) ②抑制 **biological control** 生物(学)的防除[駆除・コントロール] **under control** 制御下で

☐ **convenience** 名便利(さ), 便利なもの, 利便性

☐ **cooked** 形調理済みの, 加熱調理した

☐ **cooperative** 名生活協同組合

☐ **copper** 名銅

☐ **copy** 動写す, まねる, コピーする

☐ **corn** 名トウモロコシ, 穀物

☐ **correct** 形正しい, 適切な, りっぱな

☐ **cosmetic** 名化粧品

☐ **cost** 名値段, 費用

☐ **cotton** 名①綿, 綿花 ②綿織物, 綿糸

☐ **coughing** 名咳

☐ **could** 熟If +《主語》+ **could** 〜できればなあ《仮定法》**What possible use could be made** どんな利用法がありえるだろうか

☐ **couple of** 《a −》2, 3の

☐ **course** 熟**of course** もちろん, 当然

☐ **cover** 動覆う, 包む, 隠す **be covered with** 〜でおおわれている 名覆い, カバー

☐ **cow** 名雌牛, 乳牛

☐ **coyote** 名コヨーテ

☐ **crab** 名カニ

☐ **cranberry** 名ツルコケモモ, クランベリー

☐ **cranberry weed killer** ツルコケモモ除草剤

☐ **crazily** 副狂気じみたほどに

☐ **crazy** 形①狂気の, ばかげた, 無茶な ②夢中の, 熱狂的な

☐ **create** 動創造する, 生み出す, 引き起こす

☐ **creation** 名創造[物]

☐ **creative** 形創造力のある, 独創的な

☐ **creativity** 名創造性, 独創力

☐ **creature** 名(神の)創造物, 生物, 動物

☐ **crew** 名クルー, 乗組員, 搭乗員

☐ **crop** 名作物, 収穫

☐ **cure** 名治療, 治癒 動治療する

☐ **current** 形現在の, 目下の, 通用[流通]している

☐ **customer** 名顧客

☐ **cutting** 名切ること, 裁断, カッティング

131

A
B
C
D
E
F
G
H
I
J
K
L
M
N
O
P
Q
R
S
T
U
V
W
X
Y
Z

- [ ] **cycle** 名 周期，循環
- [ ] **Czechoslovakia** 名 チェコスロバキア《国名。1993年チェコ（Czech Republic）とスロバキア（Slovakia）に分離独立》

D

- [ ] **daily** 形 毎日の，日常の
- [ ] **dairy** 形 酪農（業）の，牛乳の，乳製品の
- [ ] **damage** 名 損害，損傷 動 損害を与える，損なう
- [ ] **damaged** 形 損傷した，傷んだ
- [ ] **daughter cell** 娘細胞
- [ ] **day** 熟 **day and night** 昼も夜も **every day** 毎日 **one day**（過去の）ある日，（未来の）いつか
- [ ] **DDD** 略 2,4-ジクロロジフェニルジクロロエタン《DDTの構造中で，トリクロロメチル基がジクロロメチル基となったもの。殺虫剤の一種》
- [ ] **DDE** 略 ジクロロジフェニルジクロロエチレン《DDTが環境中で分解された際に生成される代謝物の一つ。かつては農業用途や疾病媒介生物の駆除などに広く使用された》
- [ ] **DDT** 略 ジクロロジフェニルトリクロロエタン《かつて広く使用されていた有機塩素系の農薬で，主に殺虫剤として知られる》**one part DDT to a million parts oil** DDT 1部に対して油100万部とする割合
- [ ] **deadliness** 名 致命的なこと
- [ ] **deadly** 形 命にかかわる，痛烈な，破壊的な
- [ ] **deal** 動 ①分配する ②《– with [in] ～》～を扱う
- [ ] **death** 名 ①死，死ぬこと ②《the –》終えん，消滅 **close to death** 死にかけである
- [ ] **debate** 動 ①討論する ②思案する
- [ ] **decade** 名 10年間
- [ ] **decay** 腐る，腐敗する［させる］
- [ ] **decision** 名 ①決定，決心 ②判決
- [ ] **decline** 動 ①断る ②傾く ③衰える
- [ ] **deer** 名 シカ
- [ ] **defeat** 動 ①打ち破る，負かす ②だめにする
- [ ] **defect** 名 欠陥，不備
- [ ] **defend** 動 防ぐ，守る，弁護する
- [ ] **defense** 名 防衛，防御
- [ ] **definitely** 副 限定的に，明確に，確実に
- [ ] **deformity** 名 変形，奇形
- [ ] **Delaware** 名 デラウェア州
- [ ] **delay** 動 遅らせる，延期する
- [ ] **delicate** 形 ①繊細な，壊れやすい ②淡い ③敏感な，きゃしゃな
- [ ] **demand** 名 ①要求，請求 ②需要
- [ ] **Denver** 名 デンバー《コロラド州の州都》
- [ ] **department** 名 ①部門，課，局，担当分野 ②《D-》（米国・英国の）省
- [ ] **Department of Agriculture's Yearbook** 農務省年鑑
- [ ] **depend on** ～をあてにする，～しだいである
- [ ] **depressing** 形 落胆させる，意気消沈させる
- [ ] **depression** 名 ①不景気，不況 ②憂うつ，意気消沈
- [ ] **describe** 動 （言葉で）描写する，特色を述べる，説明する
- [ ] **design** 動 設計する，企てる
- [ ] **destroy** 動 破壊する，絶滅させる，無効にする
- [ ] **destruction** 名 破壊（行為・状態）
- [ ] **detergent** 名 合成洗剤，洗剤
- [ ] **Detroit** 名 デトロイト《ミシガン州最大の都市》
- [ ] **develop** 動 ①発達する［させる］

132

Word List

②(病気を)患う，発症する

□ **development** 名①発達，発展
②開発

□ **dial** 名①時計の文字盤 ②ダイヤル

□ **die of** ~がもとで死ぬ

□ **die out** 絶滅する

□ **dieldrin** 名ダイエルドリン《有機
塩素系の農薬で，特に害虫駆除のため
に広く使用されていた》

□ **different from** 《be-》~と違う

□ **differently** 副(~と)異なって，
違って

□ **dig** 動①掘る ②小突く ③探る

□ **digest** 動①消化する ②要約する

□ **digestive** 形消化の，消化を助け
る

□ **direct** 形まっすぐな，直接の

□ **direction** 名①方向，方角 ②《-s》
指示，説明書 ③指導，指揮

□ **directly** 副①じかに ②まっすぐ
に ③ちょうど

□ **dirt** 名①汚れ，泥，ごみ ②土 ③悪
口，中傷

□ **disability** 名①無力 ②身体障害

□ **disappear** 動見えなくなる，姿を
消す，なくなる

□ **disaster** 名災害，災難，まったく
の失敗

□ **discovery** 名発見

□ **discuss** 動議論[検討]する

□ **disease** 名①病気 ②(社会や精神
の)不健全な状態

□ **disease-carrying** 形病原体を
運搬する

□ **diseased** 形病気の

□ **display** 名展示，陳列，表出

□ **disrupt** 動(国家・組織を)分裂さ
せる，(交通網などを)途絶させる

□ **dissolve** 動①溶ける，溶かす ②
消える，解散する ③解決する

□ **divide** 動分かれる，分ける，割れる，

割る

□ **division** 名①分割 ②部門 ③境界
④割り算

□ **do with** ~を処理する

□ **domestic** 形①家庭の ②国内の，
自国の，国産の

□ **don't have to** ~する必要はない

□ **dose** 名(薬剤の)1回の服用量

□ **double** 動2倍になる[する]

□ **doubt** 名①疑い，不確かなこと ②
未解決点，困難

□ **Douglas fir** ダグラスファー，ベ
イマツ

□ **dove** 名ハト(鳩)

□ **down** 熟 **come down** 下りて来る
go down 下に降りる **slow down** 速
度を落とす

□ **Down syndrome** ダウン症，ダ
ウン症候群

□ **Dr.** 名~博士，《医者に対して》~先
生

□ **dragonfly** 名トンボ《昆虫》

□ **drained** 熟 **well drained** 水はけ
が良い，排水が良い

□ **drama** 名劇，演劇，ドラマ，劇的な
事件

□ **dramatically** 副劇的に，芝居が
かったしぐさで

□ **dried** 形乾燥した

□ **drinking water** 飲料水，飲用水

□ **driving** 名運転

□ **drug** 名薬，麻薬，麻酔薬

□ **dry-cleaning** 名ドライクリーニ
ング

□ **due** 形予定された，期日のきている，
支払われるべき **due to** ~によって，
~が原因で

□ **dug** 動dig(掘る)の過去，過去分詞

□ **dump** 動(ごみなどを)どさっと捨
てる，落とす

□ **dust** 名ちり，ほこり，ごみ，粉 動

A
B
C
D
E
F
G
H
J
K
L
M
N
O
P
Q
R
S
T
U
V
W
X
Y
Z

ちり[ほこり]を払う

- □ **Dutch** 形オランダ(語・人)の 名①オランダ人 ②オランダ語
- □ **dying** 形死にかかっている，消えそうな

E

- □ **each other** お互いに
- □ **eagle** 名ワシ(鷲)
- □ **eaglet** 名ワシの子
- □ **earth** 熟 on earth 地球上で，この世で
- □ **earthworm** 名ミミズ
- □ **easily** 副①容易に，たやすく，苦もなく ②気楽に
- □ **eastern** 形①東方の，東向きの ②東洋の，東洋風の
- □ **ecologist** 名生態学者，環境保護活動家
- □ **ecology** 名生態学，生態，環境，エコロジー
- □ **economic** 形経済学の，経済上の
- □ **economical** 形①経済的な ②倹約する，むだ使いしない
- □ **ecosystem** 名生態系
- □ **Edward Knipling** エドワード・ニプリング《アメリカ合衆国の昆虫学者で，昆虫に対する生物学的な制御手法としてステリライト昆虫(不妊昆虫)を用いた方法を開発した。1909~2000》
- □ **effect** 名影響，効果，結果 side effect (薬などの)副作用，副次的影響
- □ **effective** 形効果的である，有効である
- □ **egg sack** 卵塊《魚類，両生類や昆虫類にみられる複数の卵のかたまり。同時に産卵された卵が卵膜などにより一つの塊状となっているもの》
- □ **egotistical** 形自己中心的な，尊大

な，傲慢な

- □ **electric** 形電気の，電動の
- □ **electric charge** 電荷
- □ **element** 名要素，成分，元素
- □ **elm** 名ニレ(楡)
- □ **enable** 動(~することを)可能にする，容易にする
- □ **end** 熟 at the end of ~の終わりに in the end とうとう，結局，ついに
- □ **endless** 形終わりのない，無限の
- □ **endrin** エンドリン《有機塩素系の農薬で，特に害虫駆除に使用された》
- □ **endure** 動①我慢する，耐え忍ぶ ②持ちこたえる
- □ **enemy** 名敵
- □ **energy-creating** 形エネルギーを生み出す
- □ **engine** 名エンジン，機関，(精巧な)機械装置
- □ **England** 名①イングランド ②英国
- □ **enough to do** ~するのに十分な
- □ **ensure** 動確実にする，保証する
- □ **entomologist** 名昆虫学者
- □ **environment** 名①環境 ②周囲(の状況)，情勢
- □ **environmental** 形①環境の，周囲の ②環境保護の
- □ **enzyme** 名酵素
- □ **era** 名時代，年代
- □ **escape** 動逃げる，免れる，もれる
- □ **Eskimo** 名エスキモー族
- □ **estimate** 動①見積もる ②評価する
- □ **estrogen** 名エストロゲン，女性ホルモン物質
- □ **estuary** 名(大きな川の)河口，入江
- □ **Eugene Rabinowitch** ユージーン・ラビノヴィッチ《アメリカ合衆国の物理学者で，主に光合成や生物物

理学において知られる。1901–1973》

- [ ] **Europe** 名ヨーロッパ
- [ ] **European** 名ヨーロッパ人 形ヨーロッパ(人)の
- [ ] **even if** たとえ〜でも
- [ ] **even though** 〜であるけれども, 〜にもかかわらず
- [ ] **evergreen** 形常緑の
- [ ] **every day** 毎日
- [ ] **every other** 他のすべての
- [ ] **every time** 〜するときはいつも
- [ ] **everyone** 代誰でも, 皆
- [ ] **everything** 代すべてのこと[もの] 何でも 何もかも
- [ ] **everywhere** 副どこにいても, いたるところに
- [ ] **evil** 形①邪悪な ②有害な, 不吉な
- [ ] **evolve** 動進化する[させる], 発展する[させる]
- [ ] **examination** 名試験, 審査, 検査, 診察
- [ ] **example** 熟 for example たとえば
- [ ] **exception** 名例外, 除外, 異論
- [ ] **excited** 形興奮した, わくわくした
- [ ] **exercise** 名①運動, 体操 ②練習
- [ ] **exist** 動存在する, 生存する, ある, いる
- [ ] **expect** 動予期[予測]する, (当然のこととして)期待する
- [ ] **experiment** 名実験, 試み
- [ ] **expert** 名専門家, 熟練者, エキスパート
- [ ] **explanation** 名①説明, 解説, 釈明 ②解釈, 意味
- [ ] **explosion** 名爆発, 急増
- [ ] **extraordinary** 形異常な, 並はずれた, 驚くべき
- [ ] **extreme** 形極端な, 極度の, いちばん端の

- [ ] **extremely** 副非常に, 極度に

F

- [ ] **fable** 名寓話
- [ ] **fabric** 名①織物, 生地 ②構造
- [ ] **fabric of life** 生活構造
- [ ] **facility** 名①《-ties》施設, 設備 ②器用さ, 容易さ
- [ ] **fact** 熟 in fact つまり, 実は, 要するに
- [ ] **factor** 名要因, 要素, 因子
- [ ] **factory** 名工場, 製造所
- [ ] **fail** 動①失敗する, 落第する[させる] ②《- to 〜》〜し損なう, 〜できない ③失望させる
- [ ] **failure** 名①失敗, 落第 ②不足, 欠乏 ③停止, 減退
- [ ] **faint** 動気絶する
- [ ] **fairly** 副①公平に ②かなり, 相当に
- [ ] **fallen** 形落ちた, 倒れた
- [ ] **fallout** 名放射性降下物
- [ ] **false** 形うその, 間違った, にせの, 不誠実な
- [ ] **familiar** 形①親しい, 親密な ②《be - with 〜》〜に精通している ③普通の, いつもの, おなじみの
- [ ] **famous for** 《be - 》〜で有名である
- [ ] **far** 熟 as far as 〜と同じくらい遠く, 〜まで, 〜する限り(では) far away 遠く離れて how far どのくらいの距離か so far 今までのところ, これまでは
- [ ] **farmer** 名農民, 農場経営者
- [ ] **farming** 名農業, 農作業
- [ ] **farmland** 名農地
- [ ] **farther** 副もっと遠く, さらに先に
- [ ] **farthest** 形(程度が)最も高い[進んだ]

A B C D E F G H I J K L M N O P Q R S T U V W X Y Z

□ **fat** 名 脂肪, 肥満

□ **fatty** 形 脂っこい, 脂肪質の

□ **FDA** 略 米国食品医薬品局（US Food and Drug Administration）

□ **fear** 動 ①恐れる ②心配する

□ **fed** 動 feed（食物を与える）の過去, 過去分詞

□ **feed** 動 ①食物を与える ②供給する feed on ～を餌にする

□ **feel better** 気分がよくなる

□ **female** 形 女性の, 婦人の, 雌の 名 婦人, 雌

□ **fermentation** 名 発酵 fermentation rate 発酵率［速度］

□ **fertilize** 動 肥沃にする, 豊かにする

□ **fever** 名 ①熱, 熱狂 ②熱病

□ **fiddler crab** シオマネキ

□ **field testing** 野外試験

□ **fight back** 反撃に転じる, 応戦する

□ **filled with** 《be –》～でいっぱいになる

□ **final** 形 最後の, 決定的な

□ **find one's way** たどり着く

□ **find out** 見つけ出す, 気がつく, 知る, 調べる, 解明する

□ **finding** 動 find（見つける）の現在分詞 名 ①発見 ②《-s》発見物, 調査結果

□ **Finland** 名 フィンランド《国名》

□ **fir** 名 モミ（樅）

□ **fire ant** ヒアリ

□ **fireplace** 名 暖炉

□ **fish-eating** 形 魚食の

□ **fisherman** 名 漁師,（趣味の）釣り人

□ **fishermen** 名 fisherman（漁師）の複数

□ **fishery** 名 漁業, 水産業

□ **fishing boat** 漁船

□ **fishless** 形 魚のいない

□ **fit** 形 ①合う, 適合した ②体の調子がよい 動 合致［適合］する, 合致させる

□ **fix** 動 ①固定する［させる］②修理する ③決定する ④用意する, 整える

□ **flea** 名 ノミ

□ **float** 動 ①浮く, 浮かぶ ②漂流する

□ **Florida** 名 フロリダ州

□ **flour moth** コクガの一種

□ **fluffy** 形 ふわふわした, 柔らかい

□ **fluoride** 名 フッ化物《フッ素（fluorine）と他の元素との結合した化合物》

□ **fly over** 飛び超える, 上空を飛ぶ

□ **flying insect** 飛翔昆虫

□ **focus** 動 ①焦点を合わせる ②（関心・注意を）集中させる

□ **following** 形 《the –》次の, 次に続く

□ **food additive** 食品添加物

□ **food chain** 食物連鎖

□ **for** 熟 be famous for ～で有名である for example たとえば for some reason なんらかの理由で, どういうわけか for sure 確かに for years 何年も It is ～ for someone to …（人）が…するのは～だ look for ～を探す

□ **force** 名 力, 勢い

□ **forceful** 形 力強い, 説得力のある

□ **forest floor** 林床

□ **form** 名 ①形, 形式 ②書式 動 形づくる

□ **formal** 形 正式の, 公式の, 形式的な, 格式ばった

□ **forward** 副 ①前方に ②将来に向けて ③先へ, 進んで look forward to ～を期待する

□ **fox** 名 キツネ

136

Word List

□ **French** 形フランス（人・語）の 图①フランス語 ②《the –》フランス人

□ **frightening** 形恐ろしい, どきっとさせる

□ **fruit fly** ミバエ

□ **fuel** 图燃料

□ **fully** 副十分に, 完全に, まるまる

□ **function** 動働く, 機能する 图機能, 作用

□ **fungi** 图fungus（真菌, 菌類）の複数

□ **fungicide** 图殺菌剤, 防カビ剤

□ **fungus** 图真菌, 菌類

□ **fungus disease** 真菌疾患, 真菌症

□ **furthermore** 副さらに, その上

□ **future** 熟in the future 将来は

G

□ **gain** 動①得る, 増す ②進歩する, 進む

□ **gas** 图ガス, 気体, ガソリン **push the gas (pedal)** アクセルを踏む

□ **gather** 動①集まる, 集める ②生じる, 増す ③推測する

□ **gene** 图遺伝子

□ **general** 形①全体の, 一般の, 普通の ②おおよその

□ **generally** 副①一般に, だいたい ②たいてい

□ **generation** 图①同世代の人々 ②一世代 ③発生, 生成

□ **genetic** 形①遺伝の, 遺伝子の ②起源の

□ **gently** 副親切に, 上品に, そっと, 優しく

□ **George Wald** ジョージ・ウォルド《アメリカ合衆国の生物学者。主に視覚と光に関する研究で知られる。視覚における光の化学的プロセスに関する研究で1950年にノーベル生理学・医学賞を受賞。1906–1997》

□ **George Wallace** ジョージ・ウォレス《アメリカの鳥類学者で, ミシガン州立大学の動物学の教授。DDTが鳥に与える影響を研究し, 特にロビンの死亡率とDDTの関係を明らかにした。1906–1986》

□ **German** 形ドイツ（人・語）の 图①ドイツ人 ②ドイツ語

□ **Germany** 图ドイツ《国名》

□ **get** 熟be ready to ～する準備をする, ～する身支度をする **get ～ back** ～を取り返す［戻す］ **get in the way** 邪魔をする, 妨げになる **get into** ～に入る, 入り込む **get passed up** ～が上に伝えられる **get ready** 用意［支度］をする **get rid of** ～を取り除く **get sick** 病気になる, 発病する, 気分が悪くなる **get washed away** 押し流される

□ **give birth to** ～を生む

□ **give up** あきらめる, やめる, 引き渡す

□ **glowing** 形白熱［赤熱］した, 熱のこもった

□ **gnat** 图ブユ《虫》

□ **go** 熟go away 立ち去る **go by**（時が）過ぎる, 経過する **go down** 下に降りる **go into** ～に入る **go out** 外出する, 外へ出る **go silent** 黙り込む **go through** 通り抜ける

□ **golden** 形①金色の ②金製の ③貴重な

□ **golf** 图ゴルフ

□ **gotten** 動get（得る）の過去分詞

□ **government** 图政治, 政府, 支配

□ **graceful** 形優美な, 上品な

□ **grass** 图草, 牧草（地）, 芝生

□ **grassland** 图草原

□ **graveyard** 图墓地

□ **greatly** 副大いに

137

- □ **grebe** 名 カイツブリ
- □ **green coffee bean** 生コーヒー豆
- □ **greenhouse** 名 温室
- □ **greet** 動 ①あいさつする ②(喜んで)迎える
- □ **ground** 熟 on the ground 地面に
- □ **groundwater** 名 地下水
- □ **grouse** 名 ライチョウ
- □ **growth** 名 成長, 発展
- □ **gull** 名 カモメ
- □ **gypsy moth** マイマイガ

H

- □ **H.J. Muller** ハーマン・J・ミュラー《アメリカ合衆国の遺伝学者で, fruit fly を用いて放射線による突然変異の研究を行い, 遺伝子における突然変異の発生とその遺伝的影響に関する重要な発見をした。1927年にノーベル生理学・医学賞を受賞。1890–1967》
- □ **H₂O** 名 水 (の分子式)
- □ **habit** 名 習慣, 癖, 気質
- □ **half-truth** 名 (あざむくための)一部だけ真実の言葉, 半端な真実
- □ **hand** 熟 on the other hand 一方, 他方では
- □ **handle** 名 取っ手, 握り 動 ①手を触れる ②操縦する, 取り扱う
- □ **happen to** たまたま〜する, 偶然〜する
- □ **hard to** 〜し難い
- □ **hardly** 副 ①ほとんど〜でない, わずかに ②厳しく, かろうじて can hardly とても〜できない
- □ **harm** 動 傷つける, 損なう
- □ **harmful** 形 害を及ぼす, 有害な
- □ **harmless** 形 無害の, 安全な
- □ **harmony** 名 調和, 一致, ハーモニー

- □ **harvest** 名 ①収穫(物), 刈り入れ ②成果, 報い
- □ **hatch** 動 (ひなを)かえす, (ひなが)かえる
- □ **have** 熟 don't have to 〜する必要はない have a baby 赤ちゃんを産む have to do with 〜と関係がある will have done 〜してしまっているだろう《未来完了形》
- □ **havoc** 名 大破壊, 大惨事
- □ **hawk** 名 タカ
- □ **Hawk Mountain** ホーク・マウンテン《ペンシルベニア州に位置する自然保護区であり, 特に猛禽類(ハヤブサなどの鳥類)の観察が行われることで知られている》
- □ **hay** 名 干し草
- □ **Health Commissioner** 衛生局長
- □ **healthy** 形 健康な, 健全な, 健康によい
- □ **heated** 形 暖められた, 暖房の効いた
- □ **helpful** 形 役に立つ, 参考になる
- □ **hemlock** 名 アメリカツガ (またはカナダツガ)
- □ **hepatitis** 名 肝臓炎, 肝炎
- □ **heptachlor** 名 ヘプタクロール《有機塩素系の農薬で, 害虫駆除などに広く使用された》
- □ **herbicide** 名 除草剤
- □ **heron** 名 サギ
- □ **hexachloride** 名 六塩化物《元素が六つのクロロ (chloro) 原子と結合している化合物》
- □ **hidden** 形 隠れた, 秘密の
- □ **highly** 副 ①大いに, 非常に ②高度に, 高位に ③高く評価して, 高価で
- □ **hint** 名 暗示, ヒント, 気配
- □ **Hiroshima** 名 広島

□ **holding pond** 溜池

□ **honeybee** 图ミツバチ

□ **honor** 動尊敬する, 栄誉を与える

□ **hop** 图ホップ《クワ科多年生の草の総称》

□ **hopeful** 厖希望に満ちた, 望みを抱いて(いる), 有望な

□ **hopeless** 厖①希望のない, 絶望的な ②勝ち目のない

□ **horrified** 厖怖がって, 恐怖に襲われて

□ **hose** 图ホース

□ **hospitalize** 動入院させる

□ **host** 動宿す

□ **House of Commons** 庶民院《英国》

□ **housefly** 图イエバエ

□ **housewife** 图主婦

□ **how far** どのくらいの距離か

□ **however** 接けれども, だが

□ **Hueper** ヴィルヘルム・カール・ヒューパー(Wilhelm Carl Hueper)《ドイツ生まれのアメリカの癌学者。環境および職業の発がん性の研究で知られ, 特に発がん性化学物質の影響に焦点を当て, その影響を研究した。1894–1978》

□ **human being** 人, 人間

□ **human-made** 厖人工の

□ **humble** 厖つつましい, 粗末な

□ **hundreds of** 何百もの~

□ **hunt** 動狩る, 狩りをする

□ **hydrocarbon** 图炭化水素《炭素と水素だけでできた化合物の総称》

□ **hydrogen** 图水素

I

□ **Idaho** 图アイダホ州

□ **identify** 動①(本人・同一と)確認する, 見分ける ②意気投合する

□ **if** 熟**as if** あたかも~のように, まるで~みたいに **ask ~ if** ~かどうか尋ねる **even if** たとえ~でも **If+《主語》+could** ~できればなあ《仮定法》 **see if** ~かどうかを確かめる

□ **ignore** 動無視する, 怠る

□ **Illinois** 图イリノイ州

□ **illness** 图病気

□ **imagine** 動想像する, 心に思い描く

□ **immediately** 副すぐに, ~するやいなや

□ **import** 動輸入する

□ **importance** 图重要性 大切さ

□ **in** 熟**in addition** 加えて, さらに **in fact** つまり, 実は, 要するに **in one place** 一ヶ所に **in order to** ~するために, ~しようと **in piles** 山積みに **in some way** 何とかして, 何らかの方法で **in spite of** ~にもかかわらず **in terms of** ~の言葉で言えば, ~の点から **in the case of** ~の場合は **in the end** とうとう, 結局, ついに **in the future** 将来は **in the middle of** ~の真ん中[中ほど]に **in the world** 世界で **in this way** このようにして

□ **inch** 图①インチ《長さの単位。1/12フィート, 2.54cm》②少量

□ **include** 動含む, 勘定に入れる

□ **including** 前~を含めて, 込みで

□ **increase** 動増加[増強]する, 増やす, 増える

□ **increasing** 厖増加する, 拡大する

□ **incredible** 厖①信じられない, 信用できない ②すばらしい, とてつもない

□ **India** 图インド《国名》

□ **indirect** 厖間接的な, 二次的な

□ **indirectly** 副間接(的)に, 遠回しに

□ **indiscriminately** 副見境なく,

139

無差別に

- □ **individual** 形独立した, 個性的な, 個々の 名個体, 個人
- □ **industrial** 形工業の, 産業の
- □ **industry** 名産業, 工業
- □ **infection** 名（病気など）感染, 伝染
- □ **infectious** 形伝染性の, うつりやすい
- □ **infectious disease** 感染症, 伝染病
- □ **infertile** 形生殖力のない, 不妊の
- □ **ingredient** 名成分, 原料, 材料
- □ **insect** 名虫, 昆虫
- □ **insect-free** 形昆虫のいない
- □ **insecticide** 名殺虫（剤）
- □ **inspect** 動検査する, 調べる
- □ **instead** 副その代わりに **instead of** 〜の代わりに, 〜をしないで
- □ **institute** 名協会, 研究所
- □ **institution** 名①設立, 制定 ②制度, 慣習 ③協会, 公共団体
- □ **insulation** 名絶縁体[材], 断熱材
- □ **intake** 名吸入, 摂取
- □ **interaction** 名相互作用, 相互の影響, 対話
- □ **interesting** 形おもしろい, 興味を起こさせる
- □ **introduction** 名紹介, 導入
- □ **invest** 動投資する,（金・精力などを）注ぐ
- □ **involve** 動①含む, 伴う ②巻き込む, かかわらせる
- □ **involved** 形①巻き込まれている, 関連する ②入り組んだ, 込み入っている
- □ **IPC** 略イソプロピルカルバミン酸エステル《イネ科雑草に選択的に効果がある除草剤》
- □ **issue** 名問題, 論点
- □ **It is ~ for someone to ...**（人）が…するのは〜だ
- □ **Italy** 名イタリア《国名》
- □ **itself** 代それ自体, それ自身

J

- □ **jacket** 名短い上着 **yellow jacket** スズメバチ
- □ **Japan** 名日本《国名》
- □ **Japanese** 形日本(人・語)の 名①日本人 ②日本語
- □ **Japanese beetle** マメコガネ
- □ **jay** 名カケス
- □ **Jean Rostand** ジャン・ロスタン《フランスの生物学者, 哲学者。1894–1977》
- □ **joint** 名関節
- □ **Jordan** 名ヨルダン《国名》
- □ **just as**（ちょうど）〜であろうとおり

K

- □ **Kaibab deer** カイバブ鹿
- □ **keep someone from** 〜から（人）を阻む
- □ **kidney** 名①腎臓 ②気質
- □ **killer** 名殺人者[犯]
- □ **killing** 動kill の（殺す）の現在分詞 名殺害, 殺人 形①人を殺す, 植物を枯らす ②死ぬほどくたびれる
- □ **kind of** ある程度, いくらか, 〜のようなもの[人] **all kinds of** さまざまな, あらゆる種類の
- □ **Klamath River** クラマス川《アメリカ合衆国の西部を流れる川で, オレゴン州とカリフォルニア州を通る。全長約257マイル(414キロメートル)》
- □ **Klamath weed** セイヨウオトギリソウ《ヨーロッパやアジアを原産とするハーブ》

Word List

- □ **knowledge** 图知識, 理解, 学問
- □ **Korea** 图朝鮮, 韓国《国名》
- □ **Kuboyama**（Aikichi –）久保山愛吉《日本の漁船員。マグロ漁船第五福竜丸操業中にビキニ環礁付近でアメリカの水爆実験の被害に遭い半年後に死去。1914–1954》

L

- □ **label** 图標札, ラベル
- □ **laboratory** 图実験室, 研究室
- □ **lack** 動不足している, 欠けている 图不足, 欠乏
- □ **ladybug** 图テントウムシ
- □ **laid** 動lay（置く）の過去, 過去分詞
- □ **laugh at** ～を見て[聞いて]笑う
- □ **lawn** 图芝生
- □ **lay** 動①置く, 横たえる, 敷く ②整える ③卵を産む ④lie（横たわる）の過去
- □ **layer** 图層, 重ね
- □ **lead to** ～に至る, ～に通じる, ～を引き起こす
- □ **leafless** 形（木が）葉のない, 落葉した
- □ **least** 图最小, 最少 **at least** 少なくとも
- □ **led** 動lead（導く）の過去, 過去分詞
- □ **legal** 形法律（上）の, 正当な
- □ **length** 图長さ, 縦, たけ, 距離
- □ **less** 形～より小さい[少ない] 副～より少なく, ～ほどでなく **less and less** だんだん少なく～, ますます～でなく
- □ **less-traveled** 形あまり旅行者のいない[行かない], あまり一般的ではない
- □ **let us** どうか私たちに～させてください
- □ **leukemia** 图白血病

- □ **level** 图①水平, 平面 ②水準
- □ **lice** 图louse（シラミ）の複数
- □ **license** 图許可, 免許証
- □ **lick** 動なめる, なめて食べる
- □ **life** 熟 **way of life** 生き様, 生き方, 暮らし方
- □ **life-free** 形生命のない
- □ **like** 熟 **like this** このような, こんなふうに **look like** ～のように見える, ～に似ている
- □ **likely** 形①ありそうな,（～）しそうな ②適当な
- □ **limit** 图限界,《-s》範囲, 境界 動制限[限定]する
- □ **limited** 動limit（制限する）の過去, 過去分詞 形限られた, 限定の
- □ **lindane** 图リンデン《クロロベンゼン系の有機塩素化合物で, 農薬および殺虫剤として使用されていた》
- □ **link** 图①（鎖の）輪 ②リンク ③相互[因果]関係 動連結する, つながる
- □ **lip** 图唇,《-s》口
- □ **list** 图名簿, 目録, 一覧表
- □ **little by little** 少しずつ
- □ **live on** ～を糧として生きる
- □ **live through**（危機などを）乗り越える
- □ **liver** 图肝臓
- □ **liver tumor** 肝（臓）腫瘍
- □ **liver-related** 形肝臓に関連する
- □ **living** 形①生きている, 現存の ②使用されている ③そっくりの
- □ **London** 图ロンドン《英国の首都》
- □ **long** 熟 **as long as** ～する以上は, ～である限りは, ～もの長い間 **long ago** ずっと前に, 昔
- □ **long-lasting** 形長続きする, 長持ちする
- □ **long-term** 形長期の
- □ **look** 熟 **look around** まわりを見回す **look for** ～を探す **look forward**

Side tab: A B C D E F G H I J K L M N O P Q R S T U V W X Y Z to ~を期待する **look in** 中を見る, 立ち寄る **look like** ~のように見える, ~に似ている

- [ ] **loss** 图 ①損失(額・物), 損害, 浪費 ②失敗, 敗北 **memory loss** 物忘れ, 記憶喪失
- [ ] **lover** 图 ①愛人, 恋人 ②愛好者
- [ ] **lower** 形 もっと低い, 下級の, 劣った 動 下げる, 低くする
- [ ] **low-growing** 形 丈が低い, 高くならない
- [ ] **low-level** 形 低レベルの, 下層の
- [ ] **Lucky Dragon** 第五福竜丸《1954年3月1日, アメリカ合衆国がビキニ環礁で行ったテラー・ウラム型水素爆弾実験により, 多量の放射性降下物(死の灰)を浴びた遠洋マグロ漁船》
- [ ] **lymph** 图 リンパ液

M

- [ ] **made from** 《be ‒》~から作られる
- [ ] **made of** 《be ‒》~でできて[作られて]いる
- [ ] **magic** 形 魔法の, 魔力のある
- [ ] **main** 形 主な, 主要な
- [ ] **mainly** 副 主に
- [ ] **major** 形 大きいほうの, 主な, 一流の
- [ ] **make ~ into** ~を…に仕立てる
- [ ] **make money** お金を儲ける
- [ ] **make sense** 意味をなす, よくわかる
- [ ] **make sure** 確かめる, 確認する
- [ ] **maker** 图 作る人, メーカー
- [ ] **malaria** 图 マラリア
- [ ] **malaria-carrying** 形 マラリアを運搬する
- [ ] **malathion** 图 マラチオン《有機リン系の農薬で, 主に殺虫剤として使用

される。昆虫やダニなどの害虫に対して効果的とされる》

- [ ] **male** 形 男の, 雄の 图 男, 雄
- [ ] **mammal** 图 哺乳動物
- [ ] **mania** 图 躁病
- [ ] **man-made** 形 人工の, 人造の
- [ ] **mantis** 图 カマキリ
- [ ] **mantle** 图 外套
- [ ] **many** 熟 so many 非常に多くの
- [ ] **maple** 图 カエデ(楓)《植物》
- [ ] **mark** 動 ①印[記号]をつける ②採点する ③目立たせる
- [ ] **marrow** 图 髄, 髄質 bone marrow 骨髄
- [ ] **marsh** 图 沼地, 湿地
- [ ] **marsh gas** 沼気《湿地から発生するガス》
- [ ] **Maryland** 图 メリーランド州
- [ ] **Massachusetts** 图 マサチューセッツ州
- [ ] **Massachusetts Institute of Technology** マサチューセッツ工科大学
- [ ] **material** 图 材料, 原料
- [ ] **matter** 熟 not matter 問題にならない
- [ ] **measure** 動 ①測る, (~の)寸法がある ②評価する
- [ ] **media** 图 メディア, マスコミ, 媒体
- [ ] **medical** 形 ①医学の ②内科の
- [ ] **medical practice** 医療業務, 医業
- [ ] **medication** 图 投薬, 薬による治療
- [ ] **Melbourne** 图 メルボルン《オーストラリア, ビクトリア州の州都》
- [ ] **melon** 图 メロン
- [ ] **melon fly** ウリミバエ
- [ ] **melt** 動 溶ける, 溶かす
- [ ] **memory** 图 記憶(力), 思い出

Word List

memory loss 物忘れ, 記憶喪失

☐ **mental** 形 ①心の, 精神の ②知能[知性]の

☐ **metal** 名 金属, 合金

☐ **methane** 名 メタン（ガス）《炭素と水素から構成される炭化水素で, 分子式は CH_4。天然ガスの主要成分》

☐ **method** 名 方法, 手段

☐ **methyl chloride** メチルクロライド《メタンに塩素原子が結合した有機塩素化合物》

☐ **mice** 名 mouse（ネズミ）の複数

☐ **Michigan** 名 ミシガン州

☐ **Michigan Department of Agriculture** ミシガン農務省

☐ **mid** 形 中央の, 中間の

☐ **middle** 名 中間, 最中 **in the middle of** ～の真ん中［中ほど］に

☐ **Midwest** 形 アメリカ中西部の

☐ **might** 助《mayの過去》①～かもしれない ②～してもよい, ～できる

☐ **mighty** 形 強力な, 権勢のある

☐ **mild** 形 柔和な, 温和な, 口あたりのよい, 穏やかな

☐ **mile** 名 ①マイル《長さの単位。1,609m》②《-s》かなりの距離

☐ **mind** 名 ①心, 精神, 考え ②知性

☐ **mineral** 名 鉱物, 鉱石

☐ **mineral compound** 無機化合物《植物と動物以外の物質から成る化合物で, 一般に金属元素と非金属元素が結合している》

☐ **ministry** 名 ①《M-》内閣, 省庁 ②大臣の職務 ③牧師の職務

☐ **Ministry of Agriculture** 農務省《英国》

☐ **miracle** 名 奇跡（的な出来事）, 不思議なこと

☐ **Miramichi** 名 ミラミチ《カナダのニューブランズウィック州にある都市およびその周辺地域の名称》

☐ **Miramichi River** ミラミチ川《カナダのニューブランズウィック州を流れる川》

☐ **mite** 名 ダニ

☐ **mitochondria** 名 ミトコンドリア

☐ **mitosis** 名 （細胞の）有糸分裂

☐ **mix** 動 ①混ざる, 混ぜる ②（～を）一緒にする

☐ **mixture** 名 ①混合 ②入り混じったもの

☐ **modern** 形 現代［近代］の, 現代的な, 最近の

☐ **mole** 名 モグラ

☐ **molecule** 名 分子, 微粒子

☐ **money** make money お金を儲ける

☐ **moose** 名 ヘラジカ, ムース

☐ **moral** 形 道徳（上）の, 倫理的な, 道徳的な

☐ **more of** ～よりもっと

☐ **more than** ～以上

☐ **mosquito** 名 カ（蚊）

☐ **mosquito-free** 形 蚊のいない

☐ **moss** 名 コケ《植物》

☐ **mostly** 副 主として, 多くは, ほとんど

☐ **moth** 名 蛾, シミ,（衣類などの）虫食い

☐ **moving** 動 move（動く）の現在分詞 形 ①動いている ②感動させる

☐ **much** 熟 as much as ～と同じだけ too much 過度の

☐ **multiply** 動 ①掛け算をする ②数が増える, 繁殖する

☐ **murder** 名 人殺し, 殺害, 殺人事件

☐ **muscle** 名 筋肉, 腕力

☐ **muscle relaxer** 筋肉弛緩薬

☐ **muskrat** 名 マスクラット《北米大陸原産の水辺に生息するネズミ科の雑食性の動物》

☐ **mustard** 名 マスタード

143

□ **mustard gas** マスタード・ガス，イペリット《第1次大戦中に化学兵器として使われた。皮膚と粘膜をびらんさせ，致命的な呼吸困難を引き起こすことがある》

□ **mutagen** 图突然変異原［誘発物質］

□ **mutate** 動突然変異する

□ **mutation** 图①変化，変形 ②突然変異（種）

□ **mysterious** 形神秘的な，謎めいた

N

□ **narrow** 形①狭い ②限られた

□ **narrowly** 副①かろうじて ②狭く，厳格に

□ **nation** 图国，国家，《the –》国民

□ **National Cancer Institute** アメリカ合衆国国立衛生研究所

□ **native** 形①出生（地）の，自国の ②（～に）固有の，生まれつきの，天然の

□ **natural resource** 天然資源

□ **naturally** 副生まれつき，自然に，当然

□ **nausea** 图吐き気，むかつき，嫌悪

□ **nearby** 形近くの，間近の 副近くで，間近で

□ **near-extinction** 形絶滅寸前

□ **nearly** 副①近くに，親しく ②ほとんど，あやうく

□ **necessary** 形必要な，必然の

□ **necklace** 图ネックレス，首飾り

□ **needle** 图①針，針状のもの ②針（状）葉

□ **needless** 形不必要な

□ **nerve** 图①神経 ②気力，精力 ③《-s》神経過敏，臆病，憂うつ

□ **nervous** 形①神経の ②神経質な，

おどおどした

□ **nest** 图①巣 ②居心地よい場所，休憩所，隠れ家

□ **neutral** 形①中立の，中間的な ②（化学で）中性の ③（ギアが）ニュートラルの

□ **New Brunswick** ニューブランズウィック州《カナダ》

□ **New Jersey** ニュージャージー州

□ **New York** ニューヨーク《米国の都市；州》

□ **New York City** ニューヨーク市

□ **New Zealand** 图ニュージーランド《国名》

□ **newborn** 形生まれたばかりの

□ **next to** ～のとなりに，～の次に

□ **night** 熟day and night 昼も夜も

□ **nightmare** 图悪夢

□ **Nissan Island** ニッサン島《南太平洋に位置する島で，パプアニューギニア領》

□ **nitrate** 图硝酸塩《nitrateとは，窒素原子が3つの酸素原子と結合し，1つの負の電荷を持つイオンやその塩を指す。また，このイオンが他の陽イオンと結合した化合物を「硝酸塩」と呼ぶ》

□ **nitrogen oxide** 酸化窒素，窒素酸化物《窒素と酸素からなる無機化合物の総称。一酸化窒素（NO），二酸化窒素（NO_2），亜酸化窒素（N_2O）などがある》

□ **no one** 誰も［一人も］～ない

□ **Nobel Prize** ノーベル賞

□ **non-chemical** 形非化学的な

□ **none** 代（～の）何も［誰も・少しも］…ない

□ **non-human** 图人間以外の物［動物］

□ **nonliving** 形生きていない

□ **normal** 形普通の，平均の，標準的な

- [ ] **northeast** 图北東, 北東部
- [ ] **northeastern** 形北東の
- [ ] **northern** 形北の, 北向きの, 北からの
- [ ] **northwest** 形北西の, 北西向きの
- [ ] **not ~ but ...** ~ではなくて… **not only ~ but ...** ~だけでなく…もまた
- [ ] **not always** 必ずしも~であるとは限らない
- [ ] **not matter** 問題にならない
- [ ] **not yet** まだ~してない
- [ ] **Nova Scotia** ノバスコシア州《カナダ》
- [ ] **now** 熟 **now that** 今や~だから, ~からには **up to now** これまで
- [ ] **nowhere** 副どこにも~ない
- [ ] **nuclear** 形核の, 原子力の
- [ ] **nuclear division** 細胞核分裂
- [ ] **nuclear explosion** 核爆発
- [ ] **nucleus** 图①中核, 核心 ②原子核, 細胞核
- [ ] **number of** 《a-》いくつかの~, 多くの~
- [ ] **nutrient** 图栄養物, 栄養素

O

- [ ] **oak** 图オーク《ブナ科の樹木の総称》
- [ ] **oat** 图オート麦, カラス麦
- [ ] **obligation** 图義務, (社会的)責任
- [ ] **oddly** 副奇妙なことに
- [ ] **of course** もちろん, 当然
- [ ] **of one's own** 自分自身の
- [ ] **of which** ~の中で
- [ ] **off** 熟 **run off** 流れ出る **take off** 取り去る, ~を取り除く
- [ ] **Office of Vital Statistics** 人口統計局

- [ ] **oil** 图油, 石油
- [ ] **okay** 《許可, 同意, 満足などを表して》よろしい, 正しい
- [ ] **on** 熟 **depend on** ~をあてにする, ~しだいである **feed on** ~を餌にする **live on** ~を糧として生きる **on earth** 地球上で, この世で **on one's own** 自力で **on the ground** 地面に **on the other hand** 一方, 他方では **on the surface** 外面は, うわべは **on the whole** 全体として見ると **pass on** ①通り過ぎる ②(情報などを他者に)伝える **put on** ①~を身につける, 着る ②~を…の上に置く **work on** ~で働く, ~に取り組む
- [ ] **one** 熟 **in one place** 一ケ所に **no one** 誰も [一人も] ~ない **one day** (過去の)ある日, (未来の)いつか **one of** ~の1つ[人]
- [ ] **oneself** 熟 **by oneself** 一人で, 自分だけで, 独力で
- [ ] **one-third** 形3分の1の
- [ ] **only** 熟 **not only ~ but ...** ~だけでなく…もまた
- [ ] **Ontario** 图オンタリオ州《カナダ》
- [ ] **open market** 自由[公開]市場
- [ ] **opportunity** 图好機, 適当な時期[状況]
- [ ] **oppose** 動反対する, 敵対する
- [ ] **option** 图選択(の余地), 選択可能物, 選択権
- [ ] **orange-picking** 形オレンジ摘みの
- [ ] **orchard** 图果樹園
- [ ] **order** 熟 **in order to** ~するために, ~しようと
- [ ] **ordinary** 形①普通の, 通常の ②並の, 平凡な
- [ ] **Oregon** 图オレゴン州
- [ ] **organ** 图①(体の)器官 ②組織
- [ ] **organic** 形①有機(化学)の ②臓器の ③有機農法の, 化学肥料を用いない

A B C D E F G H J K L M N O P Q R S T U V W X Y Z

- □ **organic phosphate** 有機リン酸塩《有機物にリン酸基が結合した化合物》

- □ **organic phosphorus** 有機リン《有機化合物の中にリンが含まれる形態》

- □ **organism** 名 有機体, 生物

- □ **organization** 名 ①組織(化), 編成, 団体, 機関 ②有機体, 生物

- □ **original** 形 ①始めの, 元の, 本来の ②独創的な

- □ **other** 熟 each other お互いに every other 他のすべての on the other hand 一方, 他方では than any other ほかのどの〜よりも

- □ **Otto Warburg** オットー・ワールブルク《ドイツの生物学者および医学者。主に細胞のエネルギー代謝に焦点を当て, 特にがん細胞と正常な細胞との代謝の違いを研究した。1931年にノーベル生理学・医学賞を受賞。1883~1970》

- □ **out** 熟 be taken out of 〜から外される be wiped out 全滅する die out 絶滅する find out 見つけ出す, 気がつく, 知る, 調べる, 解明する go out 外出する, 外へ出る out of ①〜から外へ, 〜から抜け出して ②〜から引き出して, 〜を材料として ③〜の範囲外に, 〜から離れて ④(ある数)の中から stick out of 〜から突き出す wash out 洗い落とす, 押し流す, (試合などを)中止させる, 落第させる

- □ **outbreak** 名 勃発, 発生

- □ **outdo** 動 (〜に)勝る

- □ **over** 熟 all over 〜中で, 全体に亘って, 〜の至る所で fly over 飛び超える, 上空を飛ぶ over time 時間とともに, そのうち take over 引き継ぐ, 支配する, 乗っ取る

- □ **overlook** 動 ①見落とす, (チャンスなどを)逃す ②見渡す ③大目に見る

- □ **overproduction** 名 過剰生産

- □ **owl** 名 フクロウ(梟), ミミズク

- □ **own** 熟 of one's own 自分自身の on one's own 自力で

- □ **oxidation** 名 酸化

- □ **oxide** 名 酸化物《酸素とそれより電気陰性度が小さい元素からなる化合物の総称》

- □ **oxygen** 名 酸素

- □ **oyster** 名 カキ(牡蠣)

P

- □ **Pacific** 名 《the -》太平洋

- □ **package** 名 包み, 小包, パッケージ

- □ **packaged** 形 パッケージ化された

- □ **paint remover** ペイントリムーバー, ペンキ [塗料] 除去剤

- □ **paintbrush** 名 絵筆

- □ **pair** 名 (2つから成る)一対, 一組, ペア

- □ **Panama** 名 パナマ《国名》

- □ **paralysis** 名 (身体の)まひ

- □ **paralyzed** 形 まひした

- □ **parasite** 名 寄生生物

- □ **parathion** 名 パラチオン《有機リン系の農薬で, 殺虫剤として使用される。これは昆虫に対して神経毒性を発揮し, 害虫の駆除に利用される》

- □ **parent** 名 《-s》両親

- □ **part** 熟 one part DDT to a million parts oil DDT 1部に対して油100万部とする割合

- □ **parts per million** 100万分の1 (ppm) in parts per million ppm [100万分の1]単位で

- □ **pass** 熟 get passed up 〜が上に伝えられる pass on ①通り過ぎる ②(情報などを他者に)伝える pass up 下から〜を渡す

- □ **past** 形 過去の, この前の 名 過去(の

出来事)

□ **path** 图 ①（踏まれてできた）小道，歩道 ②進路，通路

□ **patient** 图 病人，患者

□ **patio** 图 パティオ，中庭，テラス

□ **pattern** 图 柄，型，模様

□ **Paul Müller** ポール・ミュラー《スイス生まれの化学者で，DDTという殺虫剤の発見者。1948年にノーベル生理学・医学賞を受賞。1899–1965》

□ **paw** 图（犬・猫などの）足，手

□ **pay** 動 支払う，払う，報いる，償う

□ **pea** 图 エンドウ（豆）

□ **pelican** 图 ペリカン

□ **Pennsylvania** 图 ペンシルベニア州

□ **penta** 略 ペンタクロロフェノール（pentachlorophenol）の略

□ **pentachlorophenol** 图 ペンタクロロフェノール《除草剤として使用された》

□ **per** 前 ～につき，～ごとに

□ **perfectly** 副 完全に，申し分なく

□ **perform** 動 ①（任務などを）行う，果たす，実行する ②演じる，演奏する

□ **perhaps** 副 たぶん，ことによると

□ **period** 图 ①期，期間，時代 ②ピリオド，終わり

□ **permanent** 形 永続する，永久の，長持ちする

□ **persistence** 图 固執，がんばり

□ **pest** 图（農作物などに対する）害虫，有害生物

□ **pesticide** 图 殺虫剤

□ **pheasant** 图 キジ

□ **phenol** 图 フェノール《無色の結晶性固体。水に溶けて弱酸性を示す。殺菌剤，合成樹脂，医薬品の原料》

□ **phosphate** 图 リン酸塩《リン酸の塩類の総称》**organic phosphate**

有機リン酸塩《有機物にリン酸基が結合した化合物》

□ **phosphorus** 图 リン《原子番号が15番の元素で，元素記号はP。生命に必須の元素であり，DNAやRNA，ATPなどの重要な生体分子の構成成分。また，肥料や洗剤などの工業製品にも利用される》**organic phosphorus** 有機リン《有機化合物の中にリンが含まれる形態》

□ **pick up** 拾い上げる

□ **pile** 图 積み重ね，（～の）山 **in piles** 山積みに

□ **pill** 图 錠剤，ピル

□ **pine** 图 マツ（松），マツ材

□ **place** 熟 **in one place** 一ヶ所に

□ **placenta** 图 胎盤

□ **plain** 图 高原，草原

□ **plankton** 图 プランクトン

□ **plant-destroying** 形 植物を破壊する

□ **plant-eating** 形 草食の

□ **plenty** 图 十分，たくさん，豊富 **plenty of** たくさんの～

□ **plus** 前 ～を加えて

□ **poison** 图 ①毒，毒薬 ②害になるもの 動 毒を盛る，毒する

□ **poison-free** 形 毒を含まない

□ **poisoning** 图 中毒

□ **poisonous** 形 有毒な，有害な

□ **pollinate** 動（～に）授粉する

□ **pollute** 動 汚染する，汚す

□ **pollution** 图 汚染，公害

□ **pond** 图 池

□ **poorly** 副 ①貧しく，乏しく ②へたに

□ **population** 图 人口，住民（数）

□ **positive** 形 ①前向きな，肯定的な，好意的な ②明確な，明白な，確信している ③プラスの

□ **possibility** 图 可能性，見込み，将

A B C D E F G H I J K L M N O P Q R S T U V W X Y Z

来性
- [ ] **possible** 形 ①可能な ②ありうる，起こりうる **as ~ as possible** できるだけ~
- [ ] **possibly** 副 ①あるいは，たぶん ②《否定文，疑問文で》どうしても，できる限り，とても，なんとか
- [ ] **potentially** 副 潜在的に，もしかして
- [ ] **pound** 名 ポンド《重量の単位。453.6g》
- [ ] **powder** 名 粉末
- [ ] **powdered** 形 粉になった，粉末の
- [ ] **powerful** 形 力強い，実力のある，影響力のある
- [ ] **powerhouse** 名 発電所
- [ ] **precious** 形 ①貴重な，高価な ②かわいい，大事な
- [ ] **predator** 名 捕食者，捕食[肉食]動物
- [ ] **pregnant** 形 妊娠している
- [ ] **prevent** 動 ①妨げる，じゃまする ②予防する，守る，《~ ~ from …》~が…できない[しない]ようにする
- [ ] **prevention** 名 防止，予防
- [ ] **previous** 形 前の，先の
- [ ] **prey** 名 えじき，犠牲，食いもの
- [ ] **price** 名 ①値段，代価 ②《-s》物価，相場
- [ ] **prison** 名 ①刑務所，監獄 ②監禁
- [ ] **prisoner** 名 囚人，捕虜
- [ ] **private** 形 ①私的な，個人の ②民間の，私立の ③内密の，人里離れた
- [ ] **probably** 副 たぶん，あるいは
- [ ] **process** 名 ①過程，経過，進行 ②手順，方法，製法，加工
- [ ] **producer** 名 プロデューサー，製作者，生産者
- [ ] **product** 名 ①製品，産物 ②成果，結果
- [ ] **production** 名 製造，生産

- [ ] **productivity** 名 生産性
- [ ] **profession** 名 職業，専門職
- [ ] **professor** 名 教授，師匠
- [ ] **pronghorn antelope** プロングホーン，エダツノレイヨウ
- [ ] **proof** 名 ①証拠，証明 ②試し，吟味 ③《-s》校正刷り，ゲラ
- [ ] **properly** 副 適切に，きっちりと
- [ ] **propose** 動 ①申し込む，提案する ②結婚を申し込む
- [ ] **protein** 名 タンパク質，プロテイン
- [ ] **protest** 動 抗議する，反対する
- [ ] **prove** 動 ①証明する ②（~である ことが）わかる，（~と）なる
- [ ] **proven** 動 prove（証明する）の過去分詞
- [ ] **provide** 動 ①供給する，用意する，（~に）備える ②規定する
- [ ] **public** 名 一般の人々，大衆 形 公の，公開の
- [ ] **public campaign** 社会運動
- [ ] **puma** 名 ピューマ
- [ ] **pump** 名 ポンプ，ポンプで汲み上げること
- [ ] **push the gas (pedal)** アクセルを踏む
- [ ] **put ~ into …** ~を…に突っ込む
- [ ] **put in** ~の中に入れる
- [ ] **put on** ①~を身につける，着る ②~を…の上に置く
- [ ] **pyrethrin** 名 ピレスリン《菊の花から抽出される天然の植物性殺虫剤》

Q

- [ ] **quail** 名 ウズラ
- [ ] **quantity** 名 ①量 ②《-ties》多量，たくさん
- [ ] **quarantine** 名 検疫
- [ ] **quarter** 名 4分の1

□ **quickly** 副敏速に, 急いで

R

□ **rabbit** 名ウサギ

□ **raccoon** 名アライグマ

□ **race** 動急に回転する, 高速で動く

□ **radiation** 名放射(能), 放射線

□ **radioactive** 形放射能の, 放射性の

□ **radioactive waste** 放射性廃棄物

□ **radium** 名ラジウム

□ **railroad** 名鉄道, 路線

□ **railroad track** 鉄道線路

□ **raise** 動①上げる, 高める ②起こす ③〜を育てる

□ **rancher** 名農場[牧場]の経営者

□ **rare** 形①まれな, 珍しい, 逸品の ②希薄な

□ **rarely** 副めったに〜しない, まれに, 珍しいほど

□ **rat** 名ネズミ

□ **rat flea** ネズミノミ

□ **rate** 名割合, 率

□ **rather** 副①むしろ, かえって ②かなり, いくぶん, やや ③それどころか逆に **rather than** 〜よりむしろ

□ **react** 動反応する, 対処する **sounds which insects react to** 昆虫が反応する音

□ **reaction** 名反応, 反動, 反抗, 影響

□ **ready** 熟 **be ready to** 〜する準備をする, 〜する身支度をする **get ready** 用意[支度]をする

□ **reality** 名現実, 実在, 真実(性)

□ **reason** 熟 **for some reason** なんらかの理由で, どういうわけか

□ **reasonable** 形筋の通った, 分別のある

□ **recall** 動思い出す, 思い出させる, 呼び戻す, 回収する

□ **recent** 形近ごろの, 近代の

□ **recently** 副近ごろ, 最近

□ **recognize** 動認める, 認識[承認]する

□ **recommend** 動①推薦する ②勧告する, 忠告する

□ **record** 名記録, 登録, 履歴 形記録的な, これまでで最も多い

□ **recording** 名録音, 録画, レコーディング

□ **recover** 動①取り戻す, ばん回する ②回復する

□ **recovery** 名回復, 復旧, 立ち直り

□ **red ant** 赤アリ

□ **red blood cell** 赤血球

□ **reduce** 動①減じる ②しいて〜させる, (〜の)状態にする

□ **refer** 動①《 – to 〜》〜に言及する, 〜と呼ぶ ②〜を参照する, 〜に問い合わせる

□ **refuge** 名避難, 保護, 避難所

□ **regarding** 前〜に関しては, 〜について

□ **region** 名①地方, 地域 ②範囲

□ **regular** 形①規則的な, 秩序のある ②定期的な, 一定の, 習慣的

□ **relate** 動関連がある, かかわる, うまく折り合う

□ **related** 形関係のある, 関連した

□ **relationship** 名関係, 関連, 血縁関係

□ **relaxer** 形リラックスさせるもの **muscle relaxer** 筋肉弛緩薬

□ **release** 動解き放す, 釈放する

□ **rely** 動(人が…に)頼る, 当てにする

□ **remain** 動①残っている, 残る ②(〜の)ままである[いる]

□ **removal** 名除去, 移動

□ **remove** 動取り除く，除去する

□ **remover** 名（塗料・しみなどの）除去剤，剥離剤

□ **rent** 動賃借りする

□ **repeated** 形繰り返された，度重なる

□ **repellent** 名防虫剤，虫よけ

□ **replace** 動①取り替える，差し替える ②元に戻す

□ **replant** 動植え直す，移植する

□ **representative** 名代表(者)，代理人

□ **reproduce** 動①再生する，再現する ②複写する，模造する

□ **require** 動①必要とする，要する ②命じる，請求する

□ **research** 名調査，研究 動調査する，研究する

□ **researcher** 名調査員，研究者

□ **resident** 名居住者，在住者

□ **residue** 名残り，残留物

□ **resistance** 名抵抗，反抗，敵対

□ **resistant** 名抵抗者，反抗者

□ **resource** 名①資源，財産 ②手段，方策

□ **respect** 動尊敬[尊重]する

□ **respiration** 名呼吸

□ **result** 名結果，成り行き，成績 **as a result** その結果（として）**as a result of** 〜の結果（として）

□ **reverse** 動逆にする，覆す

□ **rhubarb** 名ダイオウ，大黄《タデ科の多年草》

□ **rid** 動取り除く **get rid of** 〜を取り除く

□ **right away** すぐに

□ **ring** 名輪，円形，指輪

□ **risen** 動rise（昇る）の過去分詞

□ **risk** 名危険 動危険にさらす，賭ける，危険をおかす

□ **roadside** 名道端，路傍 形道端の

□ **Robert Frost** ロバート・フロスト《アメリカ合衆国の詩人。その詩は自然，人生，農業，個人的な経験などをテーマにしたものが多い。1874–1963》

□ **robin** 名コマドリ《鳥》

□ **rocky** 形①岩の多い ②ぐらぐら揺れる，ぐらつく

□ **Rocky Mountains** ロッキー山脈

□ **roof** 名屋根（のようなもの）

□ **rooftop** 名屋上

□ **root borer** 根食い虫《植物の根に穴をあけて食害する昆虫の総称》

□ **root weevil** ルートウィービル《ゾウムシ上科に属する甲虫の総称。口吻が長く伸びて植物の根に穴を開けて産卵する種類が多く，一部は農作物に被害を与える害虫となる》

□ **rotenone** 名ロテノン《天然に存在する植物由来の化合物で，魚毒や農薬として使用されることがある》

□ **rumbling** 名轟音，鳴動

□ **run-off** 名（土地や建物から）流れ出る水 **chemical run-off** 薬品流出

□ **ryania** 名カワラケツメイ《南アメリカの樹木で，根から抽出される天然の有機農薬が，昆虫に対して毒性を発揮する》

□ **rye** 名ライ麦

S

□ **sac** 名嚢《動植物》 **egg sac** 卵塊《魚類，両生類や昆虫類にみられる複数の卵のかたまり。同時に産卵された卵が卵膜などにより一つの塊状となっているもの》

□ **sack** 名（大型の丈夫な）袋

□ **safely** 副安全に，間違いなく

□ **safety** 名安全，無事，確実

Word List

□ **sage** 图 sagebrush（ヤマヨモギ）の
こと

□ **sage grouse** キジオライチョウ

□ **sagebrush** 图 ヤマヨモギ《キク科
ヨモギ属に属し，アメリカ西部の乾燥
地帯に広く分布する低木の一種》

□ **sageland** 图 サージランド《主に
低木や乾燥した環境が広がる地域を
指し，主にアメリカ西部の乾燥地帯で
見られる風景を表現するために使わ
れる》

□ **salary** 图 給料

□ **salesman** 图 男子販売員，セール
スマン

□ **salesmen** 图 salesman（セールス
マン）の複数

□ **salmon** 图 サケ（鮭），サーモン

□ **salt marsh** 塩性沼沢，塩沼

□ **salt marsh mosquito** 塩性湿
地の蚊

□ **same 〜 as …** 熟《the 〜》…と
同じ（ような）〜

□ **sand** 图 ①砂 ②《-s》砂漠，砂浜

□ **sandy** 形 砂の，砂だらけの，砂のよ
うな

□ **scale** 图 ①目盛り ②規模，割合，程
度，スケール ③うろこ（鱗）④てん
びん，はかり

□ **scent** 图 （快い）におい，香り

□ **schizophrenia** 图 統合失調症

□ **scientific** 形 科学の，科学的な

□ **screw-worm fly** ラセンウジバ
エ《中南米原産で，牛や羊などの傷に
卵を産み，孵った幼虫が生きた動物の
肉を食う害虫》

□ **seafood** 图 海産物

□ **see if** 〜かどうかを確かめる

□ **seed treatment** 種子処理

□ **seedling** 图 苗，苗木

□ **seem** 動 （〜に）見える，（〜のよう
に）思われる

□ **selective** 形 ①選択能力のある ②

選択された，えり抜きの

□ **selenium** 图 セレン《化学記号 Se
で表される原子番号34の元素。たん
ぱく質や酵素の構成要素として，植物
や動物の生命活動に必要なミネラル
の一つ》

□ **self-defeating** 形 自己破滅的な，
自滅的な

□ **semi-tropical** 形 亜熱帯

□ **sense** 图 ①感覚，感じ ②《-s》意
識，正気，本性 ③常識，分別，センス
④意味 **common sense** 良識，常識
make sense 意味をなす，よくわか
る

□ **sensitive** 形 敏感な，感度がいい，
繊細な

□ **sensitivity** 图 敏感（さ），感受性，
感じやすさ

□ **separate** 形 分かれた，別れた，
別々の

□ **serious** 形 ①まじめな，真剣な ②
重大な，深刻な，（病気などが）重い

□ **serve** 動 ①仕える，奉仕する ②（客
の）応対をする，給仕する，食事［飲み
物］を出す ③（役目を）果たす，務める，
役に立つ

□ **service** 图 ①勤務，業務 ②公益事
業 ③点検，修理 ④奉仕，貢献

□ **setting** 图 設定

□ **settle** 動 ①安定する［させる］，落
ち着く，落ち着かせる ②《- in 〜》〜
に移り住む，定住する

□ **severely** 副 厳しく，簡素に

□ **shade** 图 ①陰，日陰 ②日よけ

□ **shake** 動 ①振る，揺れる，揺さぶる，
震える ②動揺させる

□ **shaking** 图 身震い

□ **shape** 動 形づくる，具体化する

□ **sheep** 图 羊

□ **shelves** 图 shelf（棚）の複数

□ **shiny** 形 輝く，光る

□ **shortage** 图 不足，欠乏

151

- [ ] **short-term** 形 短期間の
- [ ] **show up** 顔を出す, 現れる
- [ ] **shown** 動 show (見せる) の過去分詞
- [ ] **shrew** 名 トガリネズミ
- [ ] **shrimp** 名 小エビ, シュリンプ
- [ ] **sick** 熟 get sick 病気になる, 発病する, 気分が悪くなる
- [ ] **sickness** 名 病気
- [ ] **side** 名 側, 横, そば, 斜面 形 ①側面の, 横の ②副次的な side effect (薬などの) 副作用, 副次的影響
- [ ] **sidewalk** 名 歩道
- [ ] **silence** 名 沈黙, 無言, 静寂 動 沈黙させる, 静める
- [ ] **silent** 形 ①無言の, 黙っている ②静かな, 音を立てない ③活動しない go silent 黙り込む
- [ ] **silently** 副 静かに, 黙って
- [ ] **silo** 名 サイロ《家畜飼料・穀物などの貯蔵庫》
- [ ] **silo death** サイロ死《2,4-Dの使用によって, サイロ内で農作物の中に含まれる硝酸塩が窒素酸化物に変化し, そのガスがサイロを開けた者に影響を及ぼして死亡事故が発生した》
- [ ] **similar** 形 同じような, 類似した, 相似の be similar to ~に似ている
- [ ] **simply** 副 ①簡単に ②単に, ただ ③まったく, 完全に
- [ ] **single** 形 たった1つの
- [ ] **situation** 名 ①場所, 位置 ②状況, 境遇, 立場
- [ ] **skin cancer** 皮膚がん
- [ ] **skin tumor** 皮膚腫瘍
- [ ] **sleeping pill** 睡眠薬
- [ ] **sleeplessness** 名 不眠 (症)
- [ ] **slice** 名 薄切りの1枚, 部分
- [ ] **slow down** 速度を落とす
- [ ] **slowly** 副 遅く, ゆっくり
- [ ] **smallpox** 名 天然痘

- [ ] **so ~ that ...** 非常に~なので…
- [ ] **so far** 今までのところ, これまでは
- [ ] **so many** 非常に多くの
- [ ] **so that** ~するために, それで, ~できるように
- [ ] **society** 名 社会, 世間
- [ ] **sodium arsenite** 亜ヒ酸ナトリウム《有毒な無機化合物。過去には殺虫剤や防カビ剤, 木材の保存剤として使用された》
- [ ] **soil** 名 土, 土地
- [ ] **soldier** 名 兵士, 兵卒
- [ ] **solution** 名 ①分解, 溶解 ②解決, 解明, 回答
- [ ] **solve** 動 解く, 解決する
- [ ] **some** 熟 for some reason なんらかの理由で, どういうわけか in some way 何とかして, 何らかの方法で
- [ ] **somehow** 副 ①どうにかこうにか, ともかく, 何とかして ②どういうわけか
- [ ] **someone** 代 ある人, 誰か
- [ ] **something** 代 ①ある物, 何か ②いくぶん, 多少
- [ ] **sometimes** 副 時々, 時たま
- [ ] **somewhat** 副 いくらか, やや, 多少
- [ ] **somewhere** 副 ①どこかへ [に] ②いつか, およそ
- [ ] **songbird** 名 鳴禽類《鳴管 (発声器官) を持つスズメ目スズメ亜目の鳥の総称》
- [ ] **soot** 名 すす
- [ ] **sounds which insects react to** 昆虫が反応する音
- [ ] **source** 名 源, 原因, もと
- [ ] **South Carolina** サウスカロライナ州
- [ ] **South Pacific** 南太平洋
- [ ] **southern** 形 南の, 南向きの, 南からの

152

□ **southwest** 名 南西（部）

□ **Spain** 名 スペイン《国名》

□ **specialist** 名 専門家, スペシャリスト

□ **specialty** 名 専門, 専攻, 本職, 得意

□ **species** 名 種, 種類, 人種

□ **specific** 形 明確な, はっきりした, 具体的な

□ **spell** 名 呪文, まじない

□ **sperm** 名 精子, 精液

□ **spider** 名 クモ

□ **spider mite** ハダニ《小型のクモ類に似た外見を持つ微小なダニの一種》

□ **spill** 動 こぼす, まき散らす

□ **spite** 名 悪意, うらみ **in spite of** ～にもかかわらず

□ **splash** 動 まき散らす

□ **spot** 名 ①地点, 場所, 立場 ②斑点, しみ

□ **spotted** 形 斑点のある, まだらの

□ **spray** 名 スプレー 動 吹きかける

□ **sprayed** 形 散布された

□ **sprayer** 名 散布者

□ **spraying** 名 噴霧

□ **springtime** 名 春季, 春時間

□ **sprinkle** 動 振りかける, 散布する

□ **spruce** 名 トウヒ《マツ科トウヒ属の常緑針葉樹の総称》

□ **spruce budworm** スプルースバドワーム《主に針葉樹林で発生する毛虫の一種》

□ **square** 名 正方形, 四角い広場,（市外の）一区画

□ **squirrel** 名 リス

□ **St. John's Wort** セイヨウオトギリソウ《ヨーロッパやアジアを原産とするハーブ》

□ **staff** 名 職員, スタッフ

□ **stage** 名 ①舞台 ②段階

□ **starling** 名 ホシムクドリ, ムクドリ

□ **start doing** ～し始める

□ **start to do** ～し始める

□ **state** 名 ①あり様, 状態 ②国家,（アメリカなどの）州 ③階層, 地位 動 述べる, 表明する

□ **statistics** 名 統計（学）, 統計資料

□ **stay in** （場所に）とどまる

□ **step-by-step** 形 ステップバイステップの, 段階を追った

□ **sterilization** 名 不妊にすること

□ **sterilize** 動 不妊にする

□ **sterilized** 形 不妊化した

□ **stick** 名 棒, 杖 動 ①（突き）刺さる, 刺す ②くっつく, くっつける ③突き出る ④《受け身形で》いきづまる **stick out of** ～から突き出す **stick up** 上に突き出る

□ **stomach** 名 ①胃, 腹 ②食欲, 欲望, 好み

□ **stop doing** ～するのをやめる

□ **storage** 名 貯蔵, 倉庫

□ **stream** 名 小川, 流れ

□ **strict** 形 厳しい, 厳密な

□ **string** 名 ひも, 糸, 弦

□ **strip** 名 （細長い）1片

□ **strongly** 副 強く, 頑丈に, 猛烈に, 熱心に

□ **strontium 90** ストロンチウム90《核爆発や原子力発電などの核反応に由来して発生する放射性物質》

□ **structure** 名 構造, 骨組み, 仕組み

□ **style** 名 やり方, 流儀, 様式, スタイル

□ **substance** 名 ①物質, 物 ②実質, 中身, 内容

□ **success** 名 成功, 幸運, 上首尾

□ **successful** 形 成功した, うまくいった

□ **such ～ as ...** …のような～

□ **such a** そのような

□ **such as** たとえば～, ～のような

□ **sudden** 形 突然の, 急な

□ **suffering** 名 苦痛, 苦しみ, 苦難

□ **sugar beet** サトウダイコン

□ **suicide** 名 自殺

□ **sunlight** 名 日光

□ **supply** 名 供給(品), 給与, 補充

□ **support** 動 ①支える, 支持する ②養う, 援助する 名 ①支え, 支持 ②援助, 扶養

□ **supporter** 名 後援者, 支持者, サポーター, 支柱

□ **supposed to** 《be –》～することになっている, ～するはずである

□ **supremely** 副 最高に, 極めて

□ **sure** 熟 **for sure** 確かに **make sure** 確かめる, 確認する

□ **surface** 名 ①表面, 水面 ②うわべ, 外見 **on the surface** 外面は, うわべは

□ **surgery** 名 外科, 手術室, 診療室

□ **surplus-food** 名 余剰食糧

□ **surprising** 形 驚くべき, 意外な

□ **survival** 名 生き残ること, 生存者, 残存物

□ **survive** 動 ①生き残る, 存続する, なんとかなる ②長生きする, 切り抜ける

□ **survivor** 名 生存者, 残ったもの, 遺物

□ **swallow** 名 ツバメ 動 ①飲み込む ②うのみにする

□ **Sweden** 名 スウェーデン《国名》

□ **Swedish** 形 スウェーデン人［語］の 名 スウェーデン語,《the -》スウェーデン人

□ **sweet potato** サツマイモ

□ **swept** 動 sweep (掃く) の過去, 過去分詞

□ **swimming** 名 水泳

□ **Swiss** 形 スイス (人) の 名 スイス人

□ **symptom** 名 ①兆候, 現れ ②症状

□ **syndrome** 名 症候群, シンドローム

□ **Syria** 名 シリア《国名》

□ **systemic** 形 浸透性の

□ **systemic insecticide** 浸透殺虫剤《植物に適用された後に吸収され, 植物体内を移動して害虫に対して効果を発揮する農薬の一種》

T

□ **Taiwan** 名 台湾

□ **take away** ①連れ去る ②取り上げる, 奪い去る ③取り除く

□ **take in** 取り入れる, 取り込む, (作物・金などを) 集める

□ **take off** 取り去る, ～を取り除く

□ **take over** 引き継ぐ, 支配する, 乗っ取る

□ **taken out of** 《be –》～から外される

□ **target** 名 標的, 目的物, 対象 動 的［目標］にする

□ **task** 名 (やるべき) 仕事, 職務, 課題

□ **taxpayer** 名 納税者

□ **teaspoon** 名 茶さじ, ティースプーン

□ **technology** 名 テクノロジー, 科学技術

□ **term** 名 ①期間, 期限 ②語, 用語 ③《-s》条件 ④《-s》関係, 仲 **in terms of** ～の言葉で言えば, ～の点から

□ **testing** 名 テストすること, 試験中

□ **than** 熟 **more than** ～以上 **rather than** ～よりむしろ **than any other**

ほかのどの〜よりも

- □ **that** 熟 after that その後 at that time その時 now that 今や〜だから, 〜からには so that 〜するために, それで, 〜できるように so 〜 that … 非常に〜なので…

- □ **theme** 名主題, テーマ, 作文

- □ **theory** 名理論, 学説

- □ **therefore** 副したがって, それゆえ, その結果

- □ **thin** 形薄い, 細い, やせた, まばらな

- □ **this** 熟 in this way このようにして like this このような, こんなふうに

- □ **those who** 〜する人々

- □ **though** 腰① にもかかわらず, 〜だが ②たとえ〜でも even though 〜であるけれども, 〜にもかかわらず

- □ **thousands of** 何千という

- □ **thrasher** 名ツグミモドキ

- □ **threat** 名おどし, 脅迫

- □ **three-quarter** 形4分の3の

- □ **through** 熟 come through 通り抜ける, 成功する, 期待に沿う go through 通り抜ける live through (危機などを) 乗り越える

- □ **throughout** 副①〜中, 〜を通じて ②〜のいたるところに

- □ **tick** 名ダニ

- □ **time** 熟 at a time 一度に at that time その時 at the time そのころ, 当時は every time 〜するときはいつも over time 時間とともに, そのうち times as … as A A の〜倍の…

- □ **timing** 名適時選択, タイミング

- □ **tin** 名①錫 (すず), ブリキ ②ブリキ缶, 缶詰

- □ **tiny** 形ちっぽけな, とても小さい

- □ **tired** 形①疲れた, くたびれた ②あきた, うんざりした

- □ **tiredness** 名疲労, 倦怠

- □ **tissue** 名①(動植物の細胞の) 組織 ②(薄い) 織物 ③ティッシュペーパー

- □ **tobacco** 名たばこ

- □ **too much** 過度の

- □ **topic** 名話題, 見出し

- □ **toxaphene** 名トキサフェン《かつて農業用途で使用された有機塩素系の農薬》

- □ **track** 名①通った跡 ②競走路, 軌道, トラック railroad track 鉄道線路

- □ **traditional** 形伝統的な

- □ **tragedy** 名悲劇, 惨劇

- □ **traveler** 名旅行者

- □ **treat** 動①扱う ②治療する ③おごる

- □ **treatment** 名①取り扱い, 待遇 ②治療 (法)

- □ **treetop** 名こずえ, 木のてっぺん

- □ **trial** 名試み, 試験

- □ **tried** 動 try (試みる) の過去, 過去分詞

- □ **triphosphate** 名三リン酸塩《リン酸 (phosphate) が3つ結合したイオンで, ATPなどの生物学的な重要な分子に見られる構造の一部》

- □ **trout** 名マス (鱒)

- □ **truly** 副①全く, 本当に, 真に ②心から, 誠実に

- □ **tsetse fly** ツェツェバエ《アフリカに生息する吸血性のハエの総称。ヒトや家畜にアフリカトリパノソーマ症 (眠り病やナガナ病) を引き起こすトリパノソーマという原虫の媒介者として知られる》

- □ **tuberculosis** 名結核

- □ **Tule Lake** トゥール湖《カリフォルニア州北部にある天然の淡水湖》

- □ **tumor** 名腫瘍, はれ

- □ **turkey** 名七面鳥 wild turkey ワイルド・ターキー《北米で飼育される

七面鳥の野生種》

- □ **turn ~ into** ～を…に変える
- □ **turn to** ～の方を向く, 次に～のことを考える
- □ **2,4-D** 略 2,4 ジクロロフェノキシ酢酸《除草剤の一種で, 双子葉植物に対して強い除草効果がある》
- □ **two-step** 名 2段階
- □ **typhus** 名 発疹チフス
- □ **typically** 副 典型的に, いかにも～らしく

U

- □ **U.S. Fish and Wildlife Service** 米国魚類野生生物局
- □ **ugly** 形 ①醜い, ぶかっこうな ②いやな, 不快な, 険悪な
- □ **UK** 略 イギリス (United Kingdom)
- □ **ultraviolet** 形 紫外線の
- □ **unable** 形 《be – to ～》～することができない
- □ **unaffected** 形 影響を受けない
- □ **unaware** 形 無意識の, 気づかない
- □ **unbelievable** 形 信じられない (ほどの), 度のはずれた
- □ **unborn** 形 生まれる前の, 胎児の
- □ **uncertain** 形 不確かな, 確信がない
- □ **unclear** 形 明確でない, はっきりしない
- □ **uncontrolled** 形 制御されていない, 野放しの
- □ **under control** 制御下で
- □ **underestimated** 形 少なく見積もって
- □ **underground** 形 地下の [にある]
- □ **underground sea** 地下の海《地下水脈や地下水域を指した比喩表現》
- □ **underproduction** 名 生産不足

- □ **understandably** 副 当然の [もっともな] ことだが
- □ **understanding** 名 理解, 意見の一致, 了解
- □ **underwater** 形 水面下で, 水中で
- □ **undeveloped** 形 未発達の
- □ **undiscovered** 形 発見されていない, 未発見の
- □ **unfortunately** 副 不幸にも, 運悪く
- □ **unintentionally** 副 故意ではなく
- □ **unique** 形 唯一の, ユニークな, 独自の
- □ **United States** (アメリカ) 合衆国
- □ **United States Forest Service** 米国農務省林野部
- □ **university** 名 (総合) 大学
- □ **unknown** 形 知られていない, 不明の
- □ **unlike** 前 ～と違って
- □ **unlimited** 形 無限の, 果てしない
- □ **unrelated** 形 関係のない, 親類でない
- □ **unsafe** 形 危険な, 安全でない
- □ **unseen** 形 目に見えない
- □ **unsuitable** 形 不適当な, 似合わない
- □ **unthinking** 形 思慮のない [に欠ける]
- □ **unusually** 副 異常に, 珍しく
- □ **unwanted** 形 求められていない, 不必要な, 望まない
- □ **unwilling** 形 気が進まない, 不本意の
- □ **up** 熟 **get passed up** ～が上に伝えられる **give up** あきらめる, やめる, 引き渡す **pass up** 下から～を渡す **pick up** 拾い上げる **show up** 顔を出す, 現れる **stick up** 上に突き出る **up to** ～まで, ～に至るまで, ～に匹

敵して **up to now** これまで

□ **upper** 形 上の, 上位の, 北方の

□ **upstream** 形 川上の, 流れをさかのぼって

□ **urethane** 名 ウレタン《化学的にはポリウレタンとも呼ばれる合成ポリマーの一種。柔軟性があり, 耐化学性や強度もあるため, クッション材や断熱材, 接着剤や塗料などさまざまな用途に使用される》

□ **urgently** 副 緊急に, しきりに

□ **us** 熟 **let us** どうか私たちに~させてください

□ **US Department of Agriculture** アメリカ合衆国農務省

□ **US Food and Drug Administration (FDA)** 米国食品医薬品局

□ **US Public Health Service** アメリカ合衆国公衆衛生局

□ **usable** 形 使用可能な, 有効な, 使いものになる

□ **use** 熟 **What possible use could be made** どんな利用法がありえるだろうか

□ **used** 動 ①use (使う) の過去, 過去分詞 ②《 – to》よく~したものだ, 以前は - であった 形 ①慣れている, 《get [become] – to》~に慣れてくる ②使われた, 中古の

V

□ **value** 名 価値, 値打ち, 価格 動 評価する, 値をつける, 大切にする

□ **variation** 名 変化, 変化に富むこと, ばらつき

□ **variety** 名 ①変化, 多様性, 寄せ集め ②種類

□ **various** 形 変化に富んだ, さまざまの, たくさんの

□ **vegetable** 名 ①野菜, 青物 ②植

物 状態の患者

□ **vehicle** 名 乗り物, 車, 車両

□ **Venezuela** 名 ベネズエラ《国名》

□ **venom** 名 毒

□ **veterinarian** 名 獣医

□ **victim** 名 犠牲者, 被害者

□ **vine** 名 ブドウの木, ツル植物の茎

□ **vital** 形 ①活気のある, 生き生きとした ②きわめて重要な

□ **vitamin** 名 ビタミン

□ **volcano** 名 火山, 噴火口

□ **vomiting** 名 嘔吐

W

□ **Wales** 名 ウェールズ《英国南西部の地方》

□ **warehouse** 名 倉庫, 問屋, 商品保管所

□ **war-material** 名 軍需資材

□ **warn** 動 警告する, 用心させる **warn of** ~を警告する

□ **warning** 名 警告, 警報

□ **wartime** 名 戦時 (中)

□ **wash away** 押し流す **get washed away** 押し流される

□ **wash out** 洗い落とす, 押し流す

□ **Washington** 名 ワシントン州

□ **wasp** 名 スズメバチ

□ **wastewater** 名 (工場) 廃水, 下水, 汚水

□ **water pollution** 水質汚染

□ **water-based** 形 水性の

□ **waterway** 名 水路

□ **wave** 名 波

□ **way** 熟 **all the way** ずっと, はるばる, いろいろと **find one's way** たどり着く **get in the way** 邪魔をする, 妨げになる **in some way** 何と

かして, 何らかの方法で **in this way**
このようにして **way of** ～する方法
way of life 生き様, 生き方, 暮らし方
way to ～する方法

□ **weakened** 動 weaken (～を弱める) の過去形

□ **weapon** 名 武器, 兵器

□ **web** 名 クモの巣

□ **webbing** 名 網状のもの

□ **weed** 名 雑草

□ **weed killer** 除草剤

□ **weekly** 形 週に一度の, 毎週の

□ **weight** 名 重さ, 重力, 体重

□ **well** 名 井戸 熟 **as well** なお, その上, 同様に **as well as** ～と同様に

□ **well drained** 水はけが良い, 排水が良い

□ **western** 形 西の, 西側の

□ **western brebe** クビナガカイツブリ

□ **wet** 形 ぬれた, 湿った, 雨の

□ **What about ～?** ～はどうですか。

□ **What possible use could be made** どんな利用法がありえるだろうか

□ **whatever** 形 ①どんな～でも ②《否定文・疑問文で》少しの～も, 何らかの

□ **wheat** 名 小麦

□ **wheat-eating** 形 小麦を食べる

□ **wheel** 名 ①輪, 車輪, 《the – 》ハンドル ②旋回

□ **whenever** 接 ①～するときはいつでも, ～するたびに ②いつ～しても

□ **whether** 接 ～かどうか, ～かまたは…, ～であろうとなかろうと

□ **which** 熟 **of which** ～の中で **sounds which insects react to** 昆虫が反応する音

□ **who** 熟 **those who** ～する人々

□ **whoever** 代 ～する人は誰でも, 誰が～しようとも

□ **whole** 形 全体の, すべての, 完全な, 満～, 丸～

□ **wide** 形 幅の広い, 広範囲の, 幅が～ある

□ **widely** 副 広く, 広範囲にわたって

□ **widespread** 形 広範囲におよぶ, 広く知られた

□ **wild turkey** ワイルド・ターキー《北米で飼育される七面鳥の野生種》

□ **wildflower** 名 野草

□ **wildlife** 名 野生生物

□ **wildly** 副 荒々しく, 乱暴に, むやみに

□ **will have done** ～してしまっているだろう《未来完了形》

□ **willow** 名 ヤナギ

□ **wipe** 動 ～をふく, ぬぐう, ふきとる **be wiped out** 全滅する

□ **Wisconsin** 名 ウィスコンシン州

□ **witch** 名 魔法使い, 魔女

□ **witchcraft** 名 魔法, 魔術

□ **with** 熟 **be covered with** ～でおおわれている **be filled with** ～でいっぱいになる **come in contact with** ～と接触する, ～に出くわす **come into contact with** ～と接触する, ～に出くわす **do with** ～を処理する **have to do with** ～と関係がある

□ **within** 前 ①～の中 [内] に, ～の内部に ②～以内で, ～を越えないで

□ **wolf** 名 オオカミ

□ **wolves** 名 wolf (オオカミ) の複数

□ **womb** 名 子宮

□ **wonder** 名 驚き (の念), 不思議なもの

□ **work** 熟 **at work** 働いて, 仕事中で, (機械が) 移動中で **work in** ～の分野で働く, ～に入り込む **work on** ～で働く, ～に取り組む

□ **worker** 名 仕事をする人, 労働者

- □ **workplace** 名職場, 仕事場
- □ **world** 熟 in the world 世界で
  world of ～の世界
- □ **World Health Organization**
  世界保健機関
- □ **World War II** 第2次世界大戦
- □ **worldwide** 形世界的な, 世界中
  に広まった, 世界規模の
- □ **worm** 名虫, 虫けらのような人
- □ **worried about** 《be –》（～のこ
  とで）心配している, ～が気になる[か
  かる]
- □ **worse** 形いっそう悪い, より劣っ
  た, よりひどい
- □ **wort** 名古英語で「植物」または「草」
  を指す言葉 St. John's Wort セイヨ
  ウオトギリソウ《ヨーロッパやアジア
  を原産とするハーブ》
- □ **writer** 名書き手, 作家
- □ **Wyoming** 名ワイオミング州

X・Y

- □ **X-ray** 名《しばしば-s》X線, レント
  ゲン
- □ **yearbook** 名年鑑, 年報
  **Department of Agriculture's
  Yearbook** 農務省年鑑
- □ **yearly** 副毎年, 年1回
- □ **years** 熟 for years 何年も
- □ **yellow jacket** スズメバチ
- □ **yet** 熟 not yet まだ～してない

English Conversational Ability Test
国際英語会話能力検定

● **E-CATとは…**
英語が話せるようになるための
テストです。インターネット
ベースで、30分であなたの発
話力をチェックします。

www.ecatexam.com

● **iTEP®とは…**
世界各国の企業、政府機関、アメリカの大学
300校以上が、英語能力判定テストとして採用。
オンラインによる90分のテストで文法、リー
ディング、リスニング、ライティング、スピー
キングの5技能をスコア化。iTEP®は、留学、就
職、海外赴任などに必要な、世界に通用する英
語力を総合的に評価する画期的なテストです。

www.itepexamjapan.com

ラダーシリーズ

Silent Spring 沈黙の春

2024年2月3日　第1刷発行

原著者　レイチェル・カーソン

発行者　浦　晋亮

発行所　IBCパブリッシング株式会社
　　　　〒162-0804 東京都新宿区中里町29番3号
　　　　菱秀神楽坂ビル
　　　　Tel. 03-3513-4511　Fax. 03-3513-4512
　　　　www.ibcpub.co.jp

印刷　株式会社シナノパブリッシングプレス

装丁　伊藤 理恵　カバー写真 SweetyMommy (iStock)

Printed in Japan
ISBN978-4-7946-0797-3